ONAJE X. O. WOODBINE

BLACK GODS OF THE ASPHALT

RELIGION, HIP-HOP, AND STREET BASKETBALL

COLUMBIA UNIVERSITY PRESS   NEW YORK

Columbia University Press
Publishers Since 1893
New York   Chichester, West Sussex
cup.columbia.edu
Copyright © 2016 Columbia University Press
Paperback edition, 2018

Library of Congress Cataloging-in-Publication Data
Names: Woodbine, Onaje X. O.
Title: Black gods of the asphalt : religion, hip-hop, and street basketball /
   Onaje X. O. Woodbine.
Description: New York : Columbia University Press, [2016] | Includes
   bibliographical references and index.
Identifiers: LCCN 2015038138 | ISBN 9780231177283 (cloth)
   | ISBN 9780231177290 (pbk) | ISBN 9780231541121 (e-book)

Subjects: LCSH: Streetball–Social aspects. | Basketball–Social
   aspects–United States. | African American basketball players–
   Social conditions. | African American young men–Social condi-
   tions. | Urban youth–Social conditions. | Hip-hop–United States.
Classification: LCC GV887.3 .W66 2016 | DDC 796.3238–dc23
LC record available at http://lccn.loc.gov/2015038138

Cover illustration by Billie Jean
Cover art direction by Julia Kushnirsky

To Marvin Barros Jr., Manny Wilson, and the countless others who have died too young and before their time in the streets of Roxbury, Dorchester, and Mattapan

. . . for we must "think" and the ghosts shall drive us on.
—Howard Thurman

CONTENTS

ILLUSTRATIONS

ACKNOWLEDGMENTS

This book would not have been possible without the young black men who were willing to share the most precious details of their lives with me. Although they remain anonymous or, in some cases, disguised behind pseudonyms, due to the sensitive information, I am forever grateful for their trust, humor, and love. I also wish to thank the basketball-tournament organizers, many of whom went out of their way to discuss the purpose of those games. I am particularly indebted to Russell Paulding, who spent valuable time with me each summer discussing street basketball.

I wish to express gratitude to my mentors and colleagues. My friend, Stephen R. Prothero, has been an invaluable source of knowledge and wisdom over the years and as I completed this manuscript. For his steadfast guidance and mentorship I am truly grateful. Walter E. Fluker, the MLK Jr. Professor of Ethical Leadership at Boston University, has been a vital conversation partner. Professor Fluker has also been instrumental to my growth as a person and scholar. Dr. Sharon Fluker offered valuable feedback on early drafts and continues to be a special mentor. Dr. Christopher Lehrich and I spent many lunch hours discussing my research. Our conversations have been among the most rewarding of my academic career. Several other mentors and colleagues have made important contributions to this project, including Dr. Chris R. Schlauch, Dr. Dwayne Tunstall, Dr. Emmett Price III, Dr. Victor Kestenbaum, Dr. Deeana

Klepper, Dr. Erik Wade, Karen Nardella, Rosanna Salcedo, and my friends at the Fund for Theological Education. I am also grateful to Tu Phan, who contributed the opening poem. It would be remiss of me not express my gratitude to Wendy Lochner and the editorial team at Columbia University Press for their sound guidance and expertise. Finally, I am thankful to my colleagues at Phillips Academy Andover, who offered their kind and earnest support while I completed this manuscript.

I have deep appreciation for family and friends who have nurtured this book to its fruition. My mother, Robin M. Offley, made it possible for me to sojourn from Roxbury's streets to the elite halls of Yale through her undying love and support. She deserves the credit for anything I may accomplish. My father, Dr. Robert J. Woodbine, has been my emotional and spiritual anchor throughout the writing of this manuscript. His are the shoulders on which I stand. I am also truly grateful for the poem that my father wrote for the epilogue. Other family and friends have made indispensable contributions to my life, including Peter Woodbine, Granny, Marvin Barros Sr., my grandmother Elaine Bell, my grandfather Leroy Bell, my brother Bokeem Woodbine, Leondra Dale, Polo Dale, Brian Dale, Tim Dale, Rhik Thompson, and Ms. Wilson. I am also indebted to Doris Barros, my late best friend's mother, who began treating me like her son on the day we met. Finally, I wish to thank my beloved wife, Folasade Woodbine, who made it possible for me to spend several years conducting research for this book. It is with deep reverence that I thank her for reviewing the manuscript and offering her wisdom and love. And finally, to my beautiful son, Sowande Woodbine— thank you for choosing me.

PREFACE

ENTER THE CHAMBER

Enter the chamber
this callous court on cracked concrete.

Enter the chamber
this holy home in hope of hoops.

Enter the chamber
this sacred space of sacrificed spirits.

Enter the human body
where our bones break in battle
where our blood blisters from basketballs
enter our territory
watch how we defend
watch how we defeat
how we bend, move to heartbeats
this is how we hit hoops
how we hip-hop
to cypher all of these elements
to consecrate a language of our streets
of our ancestors from the past
of our game of peace
of the first shall be last

and the last shall be first
feel our language of resistance
feel how we carry it outside our bodies
but watch how we keep our dribble
watch how we hold each other on this block
because on this block
there are shots, shots, shots
we carry all of this outside our bodies.

We turn the tables on this floor
tear it up with sneaker scratches
listen to the movement
the spins and cuts of creature habits
we jump to BASS, BOOM, and BAPS
watch us chase moon with raps
the people know our name because in this game
we fight, we write
nocturnal, we thieves in the night
we shoot, shoot, shoot
we score on the 1s and 2s
we run full, we run it back
like gun pulls, like thunderclaps
you wanna spectate examples of hardwood?
well, watch and listen to how we sample gunshots of
    our hood
so check your,
check
check
check yo mic
cus' we bout to ball hard
we bout to wild style, we bout to call GOD!
we speak behind bars, teeth onto the pavement

and spill blood until the end of all regulation
watch our bones crack, how our fingers jam
watch our domes clash, the real winners stand
on this battleground scuffed with god's footwork
we endure the pain because we know the truth hurts
so what is the message here? Or out there?
The message is that it's never clear
like graffiti, like s-s-s-smoke in the aftermath
like it's game over and what's after that?
After all the hip-hop steps have been taken
after all the ankles that's be breaking
after the noise and the reverb
after we B boys and B girls.

You may be not ready, but we hold this roc steady
we soar, we fly, we all means necessary
once children of the yes yes y'all
now we've become legendary
so enter the chamber, enter this ritual
enter where the spirits become visible
this is our church, our temple for the lonely
we no longer slaves, we masters of ceremony!
so come pay homage, give tribute to those before us
to those who have died on this court
to those who have fallen in this sport
we remember them and carry on their legacy
because it is bigger than basketball
it is forever bigger than hip-hop
and it won't stop, cus' it can't stop!

Such is the nature of the human body
a home to trillions of blood cells

which respond instinctively when something foreign
   enters its territory
they fight until death!
Such is the nature of our resistance.

Tu Phan

Tu Anh Phan is a spoken-word artist from Dorchester, Boston. Raised in a Vietnamese immigrant family, Tu shared with me that he is "finding salvation in hip-hop culture" and "still learning what it means to be Vietnamese American."

INTRODUCTION

In the end, as a bluesman, as a jazzman, it's about the life that you live that is artistically and musically shaped. And you can do that in the academy, you can do it on the street, you can do it in the library, you can do that on the basketball court.

—Cornel West, quoted in *Sweet Heaven When I Die: Faith, Faithlessness, and the Country in Between*

I have been interested in other forms of religion in the history of the black communities—as those forms contained in their folklore, music, style of life, and so on. Some tensions have existed between these forms of orientation and those of the Christian churches, but some of these extra-church orientations have had great critical and creative power. They have often touched deeper religious issues regarding the true situation of black communities than those of the church leaders of their time. The religion of any people is more than a structure of thought; it is experience, expression, motivations, intentions, behaviors, styles and rhythms.

—Charles H. Long, *Significations: Signs, Symbols, and Images in the Interpretation of Religion*

In the spring of 2000, after completing my sophomore season on the Yale University men's basketball team—a year in which I led the team in scoring and was voted one of the top ten players in the Ivy League—I chose to quit basketball and pursue my education in philosophy and religion. The decision to leave Yale basketball was the culmination of a long journey from the rough streets of inner-city Boston to the grandest hallways of the Ivy League. I wrote a letter to the *Yale Daily News* explaining my reasons for leaving the team:

> After 18 years of working towards playing Division I basketball, leading the Bulldogs in scoring last season and achieving second-team All Ivy status, I have chosen no longer to play for the Yale men's basketball team this season.
>
> Yes, I dreamt the dreams that all men dream. I envisioned thrilling, game-winning shots on national television, Dick Vitale saying "He's a PTPer Baby!," a professional uniform on my back, the glory of the NBA. Yet it was never about the dream itself; it was about the act of dreaming and the pursuit of the dream. It was about those anxious moments when I sat in my Berkeley dormitory, silently praying that I might perform in the big game that night. It was about those times I wondered if I could compete, when through tears and lack of confidence I came to my mother feeling I could not make it on the high school varsity basketball level, and yet I did. It was about learning not to play for my ego, but from my heart. It was about the friendships basketball gave me, the hope, the discipline, the love.
>
> You see, basketball was only a means to a greater end. I believe that there is a higher purpose in life, which for me is to become the best person I can become, to fulfill God's purpose.
>
> Sure, I might have been the captain of the Yale basketball team or played in the NBA, but to me those are merely external accolades which often lead people in the deceptive directions of money and fame, instead of the higher aims of divine purpose and truth. One only has to observe the millions of Americans who find themselves working each day to support the overrated ideal of comfort, often getting caught up in a descending spiral of unhappiness and disillusionment.

If my goals are to become the person I am meant to be and to be happy, then the decision not to play basketball is easy. When I look two years down the road, do I want to say I played basketball for Yale but did not get to meet with my teachers, did not get to read all of my class materials, did not go to Master's Teas, or did not have the opportunity to wake up on a Saturday morning and talk with my roommates? To the contrary, I want to say that when it was time to leave, I left. I want to look at my fellow classmates on graduation day and say: "I have become the person I was meant to be."

Deep within I know that I will not help the most people by putting the ball in the basket. I feel called to study philosophy and religion, to expose the contradictions that people of African descent face in America every day, to give my life to humanity. Indeed, there are times in every man's life when he must look at himself, evaluate his gifts, and have the courage to listen to his heart. What may seem good externally may not be good internally. What would have happened if Bob Marley had chosen a job at Goldman Sachs instead of music because it paid more money, or if Martin Luther King Jr. had thought it better to work on Wall Street than to be a political prisoner in a Birmingham jail?

Every man must distinguish between external comforts and internal truths. Every man must learn from the great traditions of northern Africa, and "Know Thyself."

So I thank the great basketball fans of Yale who rushed onto the court after we beat Princeton in double overtime. I thank Coaches James Jones and Dick Kuchen for giving me the chance to be great at something, and for allowing me to share a piece of myself with the rest of the Yale community. And I thank God for giving me the ability to continue playing basketball whenever I choose. But let it be known that it was never about the dream itself, it was the pursuit of the dream, and the act of dreaming, that was important.[1]

Before Yale, I was raised around Boston's street-basketball traditions. Copeland Street playground, Malcolm X Park, and community recreation centers were like my second homes in Boston's inner city. On those courts I met my surrogate father, Coach Manny Wilson; big brother, Marvin Barros Jr.; and grandmother, Ms. Wilson. The asphalt was a meeting ground for my extended family in the streets. During games we shed tears together, laughed, fought, and bonded; our whole lives were centered on the court. On the blacktop we also learned a street style, a way of moving our bodies, an attitude toward life that fostered resilience amid the hardships of the ghetto. Street basketball informed the confidence with which we walked and talked and how we wore our baggy shorts below the knee. The shared style and rhythm that we created through hoops also facilitated our individual abilities of self-expression. Everyone possessed a unique way of dancing on the blacktop, but there was no mistake that it was a beautifully choreographed dance. And in the flow of the game we could discover a feeling of worth that the larger society would not afford us.

Our exaggerated movements and deceptive tricks with the basketball spoke a language of resistance. I remember J-Rod, who moved on the court like a small battle tank, his face mean and eyes staring down opponents. Short, stocky, and dark, J-Rod was indomitable. "I play just like my father," he once told me. "Before my father died, he was a problem on the court. I'm a problem." It was as if J-Rod made up for missed birthdays, hugs, and father-son days by going hard on the asphalt, where he channeled his father's energy. Playing basketball for him was like fusing the past and present, conjuring his father's memory into a force that opponents could feel in every bone-breaking drive to the basket. He was street basketball's version of Derrida's "critical inheritance": "that which continues to put back on the drawing board the question of life, spirit, or the spectral, of life-death beyond the opposition between life and death. . . . Inheritance is never a given, it is always a task . . . and like all inheritors, we are mourning."[2]

In contrast, a ballplayer we referred to as Mizz was a pretty boy on the court, playing the game with the grace and aesthetic of a prima ballerina. He came to the asphalt with shorts that reached down to his ankles, clean matching Nike sneakers, and a jump shot that floated like manna from the sky. His cuts were smooth and silky like a gently flowing stream. He fluidly moved between defenders and controlled his effortless release from beyond the three-point line. Mizz's smooth demeanor and J-Rod's bulldog approach said something about their stories. In Clifford Geertz's sense of a "collective text," playing basketball transmuted private feelings into public ones, giving our neighborhood a symbolic "reading" of itself.[3]

Yale basketball contrasted sharply with the expressive culture of Boston street basketball. Yale basketball felt more corporate. Players became employees of the university, punching the clock for the monetary benefit of administrators and coaches. Coaches' obsessive focus on job security and wins and losses numbed the players' enthusiasm. My teammates, most of whom were white and middle to upper class, played basketball to pad their resumes. Practices were mechanical. Players moved through the motions each day, performing set plays without joy or heartache. Trash talking, deception, and dancing were forbidden.

Moreover, I discovered white teammates who resented my basketball style and passion. During one of our first intrasquad scrimmages, I pushed the ball down the right sideline on a fast break. A white, muscular, six-foot-six senior captain charged from the left sideline to block my shot at the rim. He was running fast. I knew I had him beat. We reached the paint simultaneously. I jumped off my left leg and held the ball seductively in midair above my head. He took the bait and swung for the basketball at the same time that I tucked it into my abdomen, switched the ball into my left hand, and floated to the other side of the basket. Our captain began flailing like a bird, landing awkwardly on the baseline under the hoop. I flipped the ball off the glass without looking at the rim—swish. I was smiling before my feet touched the ground. I expected guys on my team to jubilate as I ran down the court on defense, but they were silent. "How did they play the game without emotion?" I thought. I was a member of the starting five that freshman season, nearly leading the team in scoring. But I felt isolated on the court, as if I was dancing to music that no one else could hear. My coach explained that all of my returning white teammates voted to keep me out of the starting lineup during the following season. He seemed disgusted and shocked. I still find his statement hard to believe.

After playing one more year, I showed up at my head coach's office and explained that I was quitting the team. He looked at the large wooden desk between us and slammed his fist down hard. Yet I knew I had made the right decision, especially when a white assistant coach referred to my "minority" status to guilt me into rejoining the team. He wrote me a demeaning letter, intimating that I had been admitted to Yale on the basis of my physical qualities alone. He also claimed that the decision to leave the team would make it difficult for admissions to justify "giving" other "minorities" the opportunity to attend Yale in the future. I was offended by his blatant expression of white paternalism:

> I bit my lip yesterday about how I feel, but after giving it some serious thought, I owe it to you and to myself to tell you exactly how I feel about your decision. I want to preface this by saying that I respect the fact that you talked to us about your decision and I truly hope that you are happy with youself [*sic*] and your choice. I wish you nothing but luck in all of your future endevars [*sic*]. . . .

BUT, at the same time . . . I listen to you talk about wanting to . . . get a complete Yale experience and I can't help but think about what got you the opportunity to be at Yale in the first place.

I think we both know that Basketball was your vehicle that got you into Yale and know you are turning you [*sic*] back on it. Now I realize that Coach [X] did not recruit you here and maybe you owe him less than you would owe [Y] if he were here, but at the same time, you turned your back on the thing that gave you an opportunity to attend Yale and to experience all that Yale has to offer . . . To me, that's very selfish!!

Secondly, your decision to not represent Yale on the basketball court AFFECTS a lot of people. It affects your teammates, your classmates and other Yale athletes and the entire Athletic Administration. The way it affects all these people is because, as you know, basketball is the most high profile sport in college athletics.

You leaving our program is going to have a negative affect [*sic*] on the direction of Yale Basketball, which, in turn affects every other sport here because Basketball is such a high profile sport that other athletes often look at basketball in their decision making process. Every team brings their recruits to our games to see you guys perform and when the Basketball team looks bad, it hurts other programs.

As a minority, it also affects our chances of giving other minorities an opportunity to get accepted to Yale, because when you drop out of sports, it is looked upon in a bad light within the admissions office.

Now look, you shouldn't be playing for any of the reasons that I just touched upon. Apparently the Fire and Desire is no longer there. You shouldn't play for anyone but yourself . . . at the same time, you need to know that your decision has hurt a lot of people and has affected a lot of people. I am personally VERY disappointed in you and your decision. . . . It doesn't mean I don't like you . . . it just means that I'm not happy with what you decided.

Once again, good luck with everything. . . . I'm sure I'll see you a lot this summer and next year and I hope that things work out for you. . . . I do wish that you were with us and I'll miss seeing you at practice, etc.

His attempt to use my race to browbeat me into service made me wonder about his track record with other young black players. I began to wonder if his mentality was indicative of larger systemic forms of exploitation between the NCAA and black athletes. Certainly, research suggests that predominately white and wealthy academic institutions are dependent on poor, black, and male athletic bodies for their labor. The goal of educating black athletes is often pushed aside in favor of winning, and this has serious consequences for black athletes, who often face the additional racial stigma that assumes they are innately unintelligent. I was disturbed by his suggestion that I had nothing to offer Yale except my muscles. I soon came to understand the subversive nature of my decision to quit Yale basketball.

During my final two years of college, I became aware of the contradictions I experienced as a black street-basketball player who made it to the Ivy League. I was also fortunate because my letter to the *Yale Daily News* explaining my reasons for quitting the team had been circulated widely among Yale alums. The wife of the dean of Boston University School of Theology read my article and urged her husband, Robert Neville (a Yale alum), to recruit me. Dean Neville quoted me in his note: "I feel called to study philosophy and religion, to expose the contradictions that people of African descent face in America every day, to give my life to humanity." He referred to my calling as a "tall order" and suggested that I attempt to answer the call to service at BU. In many ways, this book is a result of my acceptance of that challenge.

I am grateful for the stories in this book for having chosen me to give them expression. The subjects of these pages "possessed" me in the sense that the literary scholar Hershini Young uses that term: "The characters, like horsemen, who mount the body, ride the body of the author and the reader, and become real in ways that transcend the traditional act of writing and reading."[4] Every time I stared at pictures of dead black youth on gymnasium walls and outdoor fences or saw their names tattooed on players' bodies and scribbled on the backs of uniforms, these "characters" haunted me in ways that belied death. While writing, black apparitions were present, insisting on telling the collective injury of race and the deadly violence black men suffer in the streets. I hope the reader will be similarly transfixed by these black spirits, through whom one might sense what it is like to walk inner-city streets, to lace up sneakers, stand on cracked asphalt, hold a ball in sweaty palms, and let the injury of race ride one's body into the ground.

THE "LIVED RELIGION" OF
STREET BASKETBALL

This book interprets the game of basketball as an urban "lived religion," in which the central problems and structures of inner-city life are displayed, renegotiated, and reimagined on the court. The Harvard historian David Hall made the term "lived religion" prominent with his edited collection of essays entitled *Lived Religion in America: Toward a History of Practice* (1997). Since then, prominent sociologists have continued to produce notable research on lived religion. An excellent example is Nancy Ammerman's *Sacred Stories, Spiritual Tribes: Finding Religion in Everyday Life* (2013). Ammerman argues that scholars of lived religion have turned their attention beyond established religious institutions and texts and toward ordinary people who borrow from theological doctrines but go outside of them in surprising ways. Scholars of lived religion acknowledge that religious phenomena such as ritual practice, healing, transcendent experience, spiritual encounters, and prayer occur in places and times that exist apart from the control of recognized experts and religious authorities.[5]

Moreover, Ammerman suggests that the term "lived religion" emphasizes the role of the body and popular culture in the study of religion. The historian of African American religion Charles H. Long, for instance, argues that black "folklore, music, style of life, and so on . . . have often touched deeper religious issues regarding the true situation of black communities than those of the church leaders of their time."[6] Our knowledge of slaves' ring-shout rituals, the sorrow songs, or blues music, all of which occurred beyond the reach of white authority and the church, would be seriously impoverished if we only understood religion in terms of a particular set of beliefs and sacred places. By drawing from theoretical tools within cultural sociology, scholars of lived religion have been able to provide rich analyses of the ways alternative communities construct ultimate meanings through their experiences, expressions, and rhythms, often on the margins of authority.

Similarly, I draw from Pierre Bourdieu's sociology of practice to examine how the central problems and structures of street life are felt and given expression to on the basketball court. Bourdieu's self-reflexive approach to ethnography and his analytical tools ([[(habitus) (capital)] + field = practice) were designed to show that in any given social arena, players do not simply execute rules but also play the game with a tremendous sense of meaning and freedom.[7] Exploring the religious and spiritual dimensions (transcendent experience, ritual, style, rhythm, etc.) of this freedom on the asphalt among young black men is at the heart of this book.

During over four years of ethnographic study of street basketball in Boston's inner-city neighborhoods, I learned that the ways the players move, style, and display their bodies on the court say something profound about their search for ultimate meaning in the world. Although many of the street ballers I observed and interviewed drew from established theological doctrines and symbols to construct meaning around the court, this often occurred in complex and unexpected ways that did not fit neatly within any particular religious tradition. However, these men and their communities did share some basic experiences, particularly the ongoing loss of loved ones. These young men and their communities grieved together on the court for their dead, regardless of any particular theological affiliations.

In addition, these young black men shared in common a propensity for flights of consciousness on the basketball court, as if playing the game had become an opportunity to transcend the difficulties of the streets. Tyshawn, a street baller, explained:

Man, it's just like you forget what's going on, pretty much, everything else on the outside world. For that however much time that you're on the court, I mean that's the only thing that you're focusing on. You don't know the time of day, everything else is pretty much you're just blacked-out between those four lines. That rectangle is your whole new space for that certain time being.

Another street-ball player, named Marlon, described his feeling of being on the basketball court as his soul overtaking his body, allowing him to perceive events outside of the bounds of linear time.

I feel like a free spirit. It's like you know how they say your spirit goes to a different place whether it's heaven or hell or you get stuck in between which is the afterlife which is the middle. I feel like my soul overtakes my body and it just do what I can do out there. Then people are always asking how do you do that move because for some reason since we were younger I see it before it happens. I get a premonition when I bring that ball up the court before it happens. So if I see it already I'll tell somebody to set a screen. Before I get up to the court I know what's going to happen. Either I'm going to shoot a three or it's going to be an alley-oop or pass or it's going to be me rolling on you.

Still other players I spent time with described out-of-body experiences in which they were able to passively observe themselves playing the game. Jermaine, who was known for soaring above the rim, likened these flights of consciousness to being on a cloud or wave: "It's almost as if your body is taking over. It's like nothing can slow you down. Nothing is going to take you off of this cloud that you are on and the wave that you are going on. It's electrifying. It's like you don't believe what's going on. You're like, 'is this really happening?' It's an out-of-body experience." John, a young Haitian ballplayer with a smooth pull-up jump shot, described being able to move in and out of time on the court as well. He likened this out-of-body experience to watching himself on camera:

> No one's on the court. You're just by yourself. Hands in your face, it doesn't matter. You throw the ball. It's going in. Felt like shooting in the ocean . . . it slows like—it just feels like I'm moving frame by frame. And then it's like I know where he's going before he even knows where he's going. . . . Yeah, I feel like basically I am watching myself on camera. Like I am telling myself exactly what I'm about to do and it's just working every single time.

Akin to the Yoruba trickster god Esu/Elegba, these ballplayers seemed to find a doorway on the basketball court that allowed them to slip between present time and a time that is "out of joint" with everyday life on the streets.[8] This book draws attention to this "out of joint" dimension of street basketball, exploring how these experiences, rituals, styles, rhythms, tattoos, and so on foster a search for meaning among young black men in Boston's urban landscapes.

SIGNIFICANCE OF THE STUDY

Other scholars have studied black participation in basketball more narrowly through the lenses of the social sciences. Their perspectives have been largely influenced by two points of view. The first reduces black participation in hoops to a psychological pathology—blacks play basketball as a strategy of avoidance and a coping mechanism for their inadequacy in other social arenas. One prominent social psychologist, for example, suggests that blacks play ball to avoid feeling inferior in the classroom.[9]

Other scholars have been critical of this "black deviance" approach to hoops. They argue that white institutions and local poverty, not black low self-esteem, account for black participation in basketball in disproportionate numbers:

> Young Black men in the inner city felt pushed from their communities to pursue basketball as well as illicit activities, because poverty had worsened. At the same time there was a pull from colleges, universities, and professional ranks, who wanted to win more games and improve their profitability. These push-pull effects created the hoop dream: unbridled hope in athletic achievement as a means to escape the urban crisis.[10]

While I have found both perspectives to be illuminating, this book attempts to go beyond deterministic, positivist accounts of black participation in sports. Certainly, black men's bodies are overdetermined by racism and poverty on the court, but to stop there is to strip ballplayers of agency and to overlook their lived experiences of the games. In a twist of irony that rivals the sleight of hand of a crossover dribble, social scientists have attempted to explain black basketball by setting aside the subjective experiences the players have of it.[11] In their desire to remain objective and to adhere to disciplinary boundaries, scholars have reduced basketball to a set of rules predetermined by external conditions (i.e., race, class, and gender). As a result, we currently have only a thin sense for the human and "lived" dimensions of these games.

I contend that by lacing up our sneakers and stepping onto the court with urban black men, we discover a dimension of basketball that cannot be reduced to an exploitative culture. This dimension on the court is fundamentally "other" in nature, in that it gives expression to a mode of experience that goes beyond words, is ineffable, and involves the spectral presence of the dead. The game of inner-city basketball is a fully embodied practice that aches with transcendent meanings—meanings that explode stereotypical portrayals of black identity. These practices often take ritual form on the court, where black ballplayers give stylized expression to the most private aspects of their lives.

In these pages I explore players' quests for identity through basketball, particularly in inner-city Boston. For four years I played basketball with, observed, and listened to black athletes in the streets. My approach is ethnographic and self-reflexive as distinguished from quantitative methods because I wanted to gain access to the felt dimensions of the game. Given my own experiences with haunting and ghosts on street-basketball courts, I have also drawn from Young's methodological approach to her "subjects" in Africana literature. I have attempted

> to disrupt claims of positivism that maintain disciplinary objects of study clearly demarcated from the expert/observer

and that perpetuate mutually exclusive categories of theory and practice, the fictive and the Real, the affective "partial" scholar and the disinterested "accurate" scholar. Ghosts point toward the artificiality of these divides, of the delicately strong umbilical cord between fact and fiction, of the impossibility of doing meaningful scholarly work if one does not care about the "subjects," and that one is always also studying oneself.[12]

In addition, there were obvious advantages to my participation in Boston's street-basketball community as a self-reflexive observer. I was already a "known" player, an African American man who grew up playing ball in Boston.[13] My status as an inner-city ballplayer afforded me instant credibility in a community that is mistrustful of outsiders. My familiarity with their world made it much more likely that these young men would share the painful details of their lives. In addition, given my proximity to the "experiential reality" of the inner city and its violent effects on residents, I could not avoid relating to my "subjects" in meaningful ways.[14] "Onaje, you know what it is like to grow up in the streets" was a common refrain of athletes before spilling their guts to me. Our mutual trust gave me access to their world.

Additionally, as a self-reflexive ethnographer, I had the advantage of using my own body to help make sense of Boston's street-basketball world. Listening to my feelings on the court bolstered my understanding of the symbolic forces at play in that arena. During one street-basketball tournament—Fathers Are Champions Too—I learned how the asphalt court could function symbolically as a representation of the collective black male body.

BOSTON'S BLACK HOOPS: AN ETHNOGRAPHIC SCENE

The 2013 Fathers Are Champions Too tournament took place in one of Roxbury's toughest neighborhoods. Gang members surrounded the court. I called Baron, my informant, for moral support. To reach the blacktop, you walk through a maze of side streets, which appear to be dead ends until, suddenly, a thriving scene of basketball drama appears out of nowhere.

The theater that is Boston street basketball almost always features the same cast of characters. There is the wave of onlookers fanning out in a circular fashion, sometimes nearly fifty feet from the central stage of the court. This outermost ring is mostly populated with gang members, hustlers, and gamblers. From their position on the outside, they can spy on rivals or scatter when police stream into the neighborhood. Closer to the court is the middle ring, which represents the most fluid demographic of this playing field. This section is heavy with constant commotion of onlookers moving to and fro, slapping fives, winking at lovers, and wiping sweat off sun-soaked brows. There are men and boys in muscle shirts, white tank tops, and baseball caps—brims straight, turned sideways; women saunter in fitted jeans, skirts, and flower dresses. Coaches with folders, notepads, and collared shirts shake hands and recruit, and ballplayers stretch their muscles and huddle as they prepare to enter the court. Then there is the inner circle. Here are older men of respect and basketball wisdom, admired for legendary feats on asphalt, eyes glued to the court's play-by-play. Older women share part of the inner circle, sitting under umbrellas near the sidelines on lawn chairs, having quiet conversations, caring for the love-needy. Everyone bops their heads to the beat, which pulsates from speakers in the background. The penetrating thump of the music is the communal heartbeat that gives life and flow to this ritual practice.

Then there is the MC (master of ceremonies) and, of course, the players in action at the center of this drama. In street basketball, the MC positions himself between the court and the audience, performing a mediating role like other trickster figures in black Diaspora spiritual ceremonies. As he travels between audience and court, microphone in hand, he uses cunning, humor, and praise to signify on the latent meanings present in every crossover, shake and bake, and stutter step performed on the asphalt. He is a master of black talk. Not bound by rules, he lobs verbal alley-oops to express the greatness of the game. And with the ball in their hands, the players are half men, half heroes, defying the ghetto's limitations with their flights to the basket. Street ball is rhythm and flow, and during its peak moments, the three rings of the asphalt collapse into a singular band, every head and toe pressed against the sidelines, caught up in the spectacle.

Walking through the outer ring toward the inner court on that day unnerved me. I had been at games like this as a child in Roxbury. Back then, young and determined to learn the game, I played ball at the park from sunrise until the lights went out. I can still remember my "initiation" into street-basketball culture. My childhood friend G-Big dragged me to the park for the first time. "Does your boy got any game?" asked one of the older gang members running the court. "Yeah, he's nice," vouched G-Big. "You'll see!" As soon as I got the ball, I proved G-Big right. I played ball like my life depended on winning that game. My crossover, between the legs dribble was lightning quick. I played out of my mind. In some ways my life did depend on that game. Every boy in my neighborhood understood that there were three common routes of escape from the ghetto. You could become a gangster, a rapper, or a ballplayer (admittedly, you could become a "student" or "artist," but they were often socially isolated). And since I couldn't fight or rhyme on the mic, basketball was my refuge.

If gang members viewed you as a promising ballplayer in my neighborhood, they would grant you a pass from participation in the gang (not so much for students; "nerds" were targets). To them, being a basketball star meant that you embodied a higher purpose; you were "Black Jesus," "Born Ready," the "Chosen One," "the Truth," or "the Answer" to the problems besetting the inner city. Eventually I did become one of Boston's best ballplayers, leading my neighborhood team to a neighborhood-league championship and earning *Boston*

Globe and *Boston Herald* All-Scholastic honors. But that was years ago, before Yale University basketball and graduate school at Boston University pulled me away from the neighborhood.

Thus, returning to a Roxbury basketball court after graduate school, surrounded by unfamiliar gang members, was frightening. Although I had played street basketball in my youth, I was now, in part, a stranger here, eager to avoid attracting the attention of gang members with my awkward body. I did what I could to improvise. I passed by hustlers with my chest puffed out. I added a limp to my step, dipping down low on one side, coming up high on the other. I tried to focus my eyes on the action inside the court, careful to avoid the stares of young men on the outside. I wore a mask of black masculinity to guard against becoming a target in the neighborhood. But when I finally reached the entrance to the basketball court, something released the burden of my facade. A feeling of relief washed over my entire body. I could breathe again. The gateway to the court beckoned me into a hoops sanctuary from a hostile world.

As I passed the middle ring of onlookers, there were children bouncing balls, some women selling food, and players stretching on the hot concrete in their uniforms. I made my way to the sidelines. Several wise men stood there discussing the game. One turned to me and pointed in exasperation: "See they're shooting too many threes. They need to drive the ball to the hole! Now you look like a smart man, right? If you miss more threes than I hit twos, who wins?" I tried doing the math in my head, "Um." He answered for me: "I do." "Yeah, you're right" I said, thinking I should have known the answer. I spotted another hoops elder. He had broken major college basketball records and earned professional ball contracts overseas. He attended every hoops game in Boston's black neighborhoods. He greeted me with a wise and raspy whisper: "What's up, my man?" His tone was cool and baritone, so I had to lean in, especially since reggae rhythms vibrated from giant speakers.

During a time-out the music stopped and a middle-aged black man with a microphone sauntered onto the court. He introduced himself with a preacher's voice that was reminiscent of Malcolm X's. As a Boston mayoral candidate and native of the city, this man understood the explosive mixture of dread and hope haunting Roxbury's residents: "I'm the type of man that can't be bought," he said. "I am a man of the community and unlike these other politicians, I care about the community. Since the Boston Marathon bombing, there have been seventy-three shootings in our community. We need to take our community back and stop relying on others to do it for us. We need to love ourselves. I am your brother. Please support your brother, and I will serve you as I always have!" The crowd gave him cautious applause. His passionate style of delivery stimulated their hopes, but their tepid applause underscored fears that black boys would continue to be shot and murdered no matter who was in office.

After the preacher-politician left the court, I stayed to watch a few more plays. The old wise man on the sidelines had been correct. Although one light-skinned, bald-headed player with a sweet stroke was shooting three pointers from way behind the arc, his team was getting destroyed on the other end of the floor with easy lay-ups. His deep jump shots were leading to long rebounds and fast-break points for the other team. In that moment I nodded my head in affirmation of the wisdom of elders: bad offense is bad defense, and when you live by the three you die by the three.

My journey from the outer ring to the inner circle was a sensual study in the ritual geography of the court. As I walked through the outer circle, I turned myself into a pseudogangster and a hustler. The streets' normative definitions of black masculinity took possession of my body—be tough, hide your real emotions, distrust everything, avoid intimacy, and "pose" with a hard countenance. My body became what Bourdieu referred to as a "living memory pad," performing the racial and gendered history of the streets. At the same time, when I passed through the gateway to the court, there was a powerful moment of release—a letting go of the burden of being black and male. I could feel my body again, with all its fluidity, vitality, and heart. In one sense, the hidden rules of the larger culture had imprinted themselves on my flesh. But by some inner impulse, I, too, had turned the court into a vehicle of self-emancipation.

These insights regarding street basketball, social space, and freedom were further clarified when I returned from the court to everyday life. I was aware again of leaving a safe enclosure, of the vulnerability of my body to the streets and their violence. Moving beyond the outer circle felt like leaving a strange world behind, one totally separate from and inimical to the white, middle-class context of my graduate studies. In comparison, the university culture felt disembodied. It lacked sensual reminders of the rhythmic communal ties I had reluctantly left behind.

As I reflected on the ritual space of the asphalt, it became clearer to me that the outer ring of the basketball court often represents the powerful socioeconomic forces (poverty, racism, and masculine role strain) that work to constrain black male bodies, pushing them toward limited definitions of self as ballplayers, gangsters, and hustlers. This "symbolic violence," as Bourdieu refers to it, is often embodied and internalized by the players.[15] But the experience of being on the asphalt court and moving one's body with others to the rhythms of ball and sound gives black men and their communities access to a communal sense of freedom that counters the effects of this dehumanization. This was one of the contradictions of being a black ballplayer that I had been longing to understand.

Members of Boston's street-basketball community do not go to inner-city courts simply to be exploited. They go to discover their humanity, to demonstrate to themselves and others that they possess something intangible—something "more," not subject to the decay of urban life.[16] Especially during times of crisis, these men turn themselves into choreographers of the court, playing the game to express grief, find hope, and revel in community. While the practices of street basketball do express considerable symbolic violence, the actual experience of playing the game goes far beyond the reenactment of stereotypical representations of black men as dumb jocks or uncontrollable animals. Religious studies in particular can speak to this deeper dimension of human agency on the asphalt, at the level of feeling, emotion, and the embodiment of what William James calls a "more."

The book is organized into three parts: "Memory," "Hope," and "Healing." Chapter 1 documents the origins of black basketball as an offshoot of "muscular Christianity" and its genesis in Harlem's black churches. Although, I argue, black basketball began as a communal and spiritual mode of resistance to white supremacy, street basketball now functions as a refuge for black youth living in urban exile. Chapter 2 shifts to contemporary inner-city Boston, where I spent four years conducting an ethnographic study of the street-basketball community. Basketball courts in this city have become "sites of memory," spaces that embody the violence of the past and the emotional toll of remembering the dead. These "memorial games" are surrounded with images of deceased young men and women, and players "talk to the dead" during games.

If part 1 explores the themes of memory and death in street basketball, part 2 examines hope and life. Chapter 3 gives voice to Jason's story, a ballplayer whom I befriended on Boston's courts. Jason plays street basketball at the behest of his great-grandmother's spirit and God, who give him the hope that he can break the cycle of violence and pain in his family. Chapter 4 explores C.J.'s search for a "second life" through basketball. Childhood friends, C.J. and I lost touch when I went to Yale and he went to prison, but C.J. rediscovered hope in hoops during his incarceration. I am thankful that this book and the memory of our late and beloved friend, Marvin Barros Jr., and coach, Manny Wilson, reunited C.J. and me. I will never forget the last street-basketball game that Jason, C.J., and I played together in honor of those who died before us.

Part 3, "Healing," explores the choreographies of inner-city basketball games, especially for their potential as rites of transformation among inner-city residents. Chapter 5 examines rituals of grief in street basketball as models of healing for young black men and their communities faced with urban violence. Chapter 6, to paraphrase the theologian James Noel, explores the ways street-basketball games, like blues music, do not make you sad even though they are grounded in and infused with sadness.[17] The celebratory nature of the games is examined—using the dunk as an archetype—for its ability to bind together members of the street-basketball community.

Finally, the epilogue issues a challenge in light of the continued loss of black life in U.S. cities. According to the pastoral-care scholar Gregory Ellison II, black men have been "cut dead" in America not simply by the deliberate discrimination and violence of a white majority that fails to see them properly but also by other black men, who have internalized a sense of invisibility and the devaluation of their lives.[18] The epilogue suggests a step toward mending this collective injury, starting with a call to the elders to participate more actively the grieving practices of young black men on the asphalt.

PART I

MEMORY

I

"LAST ONES LEFT"
IN THE GAME
From Black Resistance to Urban Exile

With other black boys the strife was not so fiercely sunny: their youth shrunk into tasteless sycophancy, or into silent hatred of the pale world about them and mocking distrust of everything white; or wasted itself in a bitter cry, Why did God make me an outcast and a stranger in mine own house? The shades of the prison-house closed round about us all: walls strait and stubborn to the whitest, but relentlessly narrow, tall, and unscalable to sons of night who must plod darkly on in resignation, or beat unavailing palms against the stone, or steadily, half hopelessly, watch the streak of blue above.

—W. E. B. Du Bois, *The Souls of Black Folk*

We are born like this, into this, into these carefully mad wars . . . into fist fights that end as shootings and knifings . . . born into this walking and living through this, dying because of this, muted because of this, castrated, debauched, disinherited because of this, fooled by this, used by this, pissed on by this, made violent, made inhuman by this, the heart is blackened, the fingers reach for the throat, the gun, the knife . . . the fingers reach toward an unresponsive god . . . we are born into sorrowful deadliness. . . .

—Charles Bukowski, "Dinosauria, We"

Shorty's slim, dangly black body twisted and twirled on Roxbury's asphalt courts. He seemed guided by an otherworldly force. As neighborhood kids, we studied and worshipped his every move. I witnessed Shorty dribble the ball along the right baseline leaning so far over his left shoulder that his torso became parallel with the ground. Without falling, he managed to tiptoe around one defender, and then suddenly, he launched off the pavement like a rocket, holding the ball with two-hands, arms and legs fully extended in midair. As Shorty hung there, we observers stood in awe. Then almost as gracefully as he glided toward the sky, he retracted his body downward to avoid a defender who had leapt to block his shot. While this defender remained at the rim, Shorty descended to just inches above the court, his face nearly touching the ground. From this underworld he effortlessly flicked the ball off of his wrist. The rotating sphere came to life, spinning upward toward the glass above the hoop, kissing the backboard and falling into a swishing net. An "Ahhh!" swept throughout the crowd; we were mesmerized. It was as if Shorty was destined to be great with the basketball.

Fifteen years later I had not forgotten those days when Shorty seemed like a god on the court. Since then myths abounded of his fall to the perils of drugs and prison. But I wanted to speak to the man himself. Then one day as I stood on the sidelines of Roxbury's Malcolm X Park, Shorty hopped onto the asphalt in front of me.

The Suave Life Tournament was the fifth street-ball competition of the summer in Boston's black neighborhoods. The games were organized to honor the memory of several black youths murdered in the streets of Mattapan on September 28, 2010. On the morning of the killings, local residents discovered naked, bullet-riddled, black bodies on the sidewalks. Among the dead were a mother, her two-year old child, and two black men. A fifth young black man still lay on the sidewalk gasping for air. The *Boston*

Globe described the horrible scene: "The bodies of two male victims were found naked, sprawled on a side street . . . in one of the cities roughest sections. The woman, 21-years old . . . had been shot in the head, and her child, she held fatally wounded. A third male also lay naked in the area . . . clinging to life after attempting to flee." A ten-year-old boy who heard the shootings from his bedroom window spoke about the panic he was feeling: "It puts fear in people's hearts."[1]

A general sense of terror pervades Boston's black neighborhoods—Mattapan, Roxbury, and Dorchester—the places where I conducted this ethnography of street basketball. According to the Urban League of Eastern Massachusetts's in-depth study, the "State of Black Boston" (2011), there is a history of underlying racial inequity in Boston that is a root cause of the subhuman living conditions faced by many of the city's black residents.[2] The report suggests that while there has been progress, Boston's history of racial injury persists in nearly every major category of civic life and physical well-being.[3]

More than a fifth of Boston's black residents twenty-five-years-old and under lack a high school diploma, and only 11.9 percent have earned a bachelor's degree. A quarter of all Boston's black residents are impoverished, double the rate of whites in the city. Black unemployment is the highest of any racial group—while employed blacks make $30,000 less than whites on average. Nearly half (45.2 percent) of black youth depend on food stamps, and households run by single-parent mothers represent over half (55.4 percent) of Boston's black family types. Black residents are twice as likely to die of heart disease and more than three times as likely to die of diabetes. Black families suffer from the highest infant-mortality rates in Boston. Whereas the median asking price for a home in black Mattapan is $154,967, it is $456,837 citywide. Blacks who earn identical incomes as whites are denied housing loans twice as often. Two of Boston's black neighborhoods—Roxbury and Mattapan—carry the burden of maintaining the greatest amount of high-cost home loans in the city.[4]

Poverty, racial discrimination, poor education, and disease are compounded by disparities in crime and the criminal justice system. Roxbury, Dorchester, and Mattapan bear the highest crime rates. At least half of all reported violent crimes in Boston occur in these three areas, including 63 percent of homicides, 52 percent of robberies and 51 percent of aggravated assaults. Many of Boston's black men and women who do not suffer literal death in the streets are disenfranchised and rendered socially invisible through incarceration. In 2010 blacks were only 6.6 percent of the Massachusetts population but accounted for nearly 35 percent of the state's inmates. Having to endure a continuous threat of violence, bodily harm, and imprisonment has led to an unquantifiable measure of affective injury and grief in this community. The 2010 national census ranked Boston as the eleventh most black-white segregated city in the country.[5]

There was a picture of one Mattapan murder victim adorning the fence surrounding the asphalt basketball court during the Suave Life Tournament. After spending some time staring at his face, I proceeded to the fence opening, which defined the court from the streets. Once I stepped inside, I found myself partially underground, as this particular court is sunk below street level, in the manner of a netherworld.[6] There, in the flesh, was Shorty. I noticed him immediately because he still moved his body with the style and grace of a street baller, legs and arms swinging rhythmically back and forth as if an invisible basketball dribbled between his legs.

He laid down his gym bag on the asphalt and walked toward me. Our eyes met—but I noticed something strange. Shorty's eyes seemed empty. I called his name: "Shorty!" "What's up," he responded softly, looking past me as if I were not there. "Shorty, it's me, Onaje." "I know," he said, staring in the distance. "Oh," I said, feeling as if I was speaking to a ghost of a man. "Wow, it's been so long. Listen, man, I am writing a book on street basketball and would love to interview a legend. Do you think you'd be interested?" "Yep," he responded. "Okay, what is your phone number so I can give you a call?" Later that evening, I sent Shorty a text message. His response was cautiously revealing: "Okay, I have a lot to tell. But only for you." What he had to tell was almost too terrible for words.

Shorty shared his story with me as we sat on the front steps of his apartment building in Roxbury. He was born and raised in Roxbury's Avenue projects—pissy hallways, roach infestations, filthy clothes, murderers, crack addicts desperate for a fix, and devastating poverty. His biological parents were dope addicts. His grandmother, an informal network of peers and mentors associated with local basketball, and gang members constituted his primary role models: "I never really had a relationship like with my mom. I always use to see my mom when she did come by. And my pops he was dead but he wasn't dead. Like he was in the house, but when we did something wrong that's the only time he said something." He continued to describe the social and familial violence that shaped his external and internal worlds as a child.

I ain't never really sat down and had a deep conversation with my pops or my mom. My mom's basically doing drugs, moms and pops, you know what I'm saying? Just basically on drugs and throughout my whole life growing up.

You know growing up in the Avenue. It was kind of hard. You see like every day drug dealers people selling whatever out there. You know, it's crazy. You got robbers, stick up kids, and at a young age I kind of like swayed away from that, tried to sway away from that. But I think as I got older it came into play, but basketball was a way out to not be in the streets.

Bourdieu uses the term "habitus" to refer to the tendency in human beings to unconsciously internalize their external environments. Born into a field of social forces, people habituate to the norms of the field, even if they are harmful to one's self. Over time these cultural narratives shape the thoughts and feelings of groups and individuals, such that their bodies become the historical "repositories" of a culture.[7] Employing sports metaphors, Bourdieu draws an analogy between this social process of internalization and an athlete's development of a "feel for the game." When an athlete possesses a feel for the game, the rules become second nature.[8] In contexts of social violence, this second nature is so insidious precisely because marginal individuals and groups are unaware of it as such.

Shorty certainly embodied the dominant narratives of the streets. However, "basketball was a way out not to be in the streets." The basketball court signified an alternative space of resistance to the violence of the neighborhood. Shorty substituted his "dead" biological father and mother with the loving family members he found on the court, and they schooled him in the art of the game:

> I just learned from watching everybody, you know, my man Kane, my brother, my cousin, all them dudes. Dana, all them dudes that played basketball that was real tough from around my way. I learned from a couple of dudes from other projects, you know, Lewis projects, you know. Bane, I used to watch him and then my brother go at it. I used to steal moves and all that. It was only right. It's only right, that's how you get nicer. You just add your little twist to it. That's what I used to just do. It was other people's moves, I just put a little, add a little something extra.

In reality, Shorty added more than "a little something extra" to his game. By the time he was fifteen years old, he was an emerging basketball legend in Roxbury. His style on the court was uncanny and unscripted.[9] Think of the way a speedskater lunges from side to side across the ice. Picture one arm swinging high in the air as the same leg dashes forward. Put the ball in his right hand and let it cross over smoothly from right to left as it sweeps the ground low before coming up high on the other side. Now imagine Shorty's feet skating between muscular defenders as his body glides across the concrete rubble. His dribble, like the rhythm of his life, was full of incredible highs and breathtaking lows.

Shorty's father enlisted him in the drug game as a child, forcing him to buy crack for his family. He hated school because of the unwashed clothes he was often forced to wear to class. Plus what would school teach him about surviving the projects? He was hungry and broke. The shame of buying crack for his parents rotted away his self-esteem. He began using drugs to bury the pain and developed a visceral sense of "nobodiness": "I didn't really have the support. I was in high school like I didn't have no clothes that whole time, from like high school on. I started selling drugs. You know what I mean? I started drinking, smoking weed, just not caring. I think high school was like the turning point of my life."

Shorty's high school administrators treated him like a commodity, forging his grades so that they could ship him off to play ball for a predominately white and wealthy high school. The journalist William Rhoden suggests that impoverished black males are often viewed as the "raw materials" of white schools and businesses seeking to benefit from their poverty and "natural" athletic talent. Informal local and national recruiting systems, which he refers to as "conveyor belts," then funnel black bodies from the streets to the halls of the white elite.[10]

Shorty experienced more shame and isolation at his new school, eventually returning to Boston aimless and depressed. As a high school dropout, he gradually turned into one of the most active drug dealers and thieves in Avenue projects. At eighteen years old he was incarcerated:

But after that situation, I came back to Boston. I ended up catching a case. I ended up catching an armed robbery case, and I probably was like I want to say eighteen at the time. I caught the case and I thought I was going to get off, but I ended up doing two years from that case and when I got out I was kind of lost. Like what am I going to do, you know? I mean, there was a couple of other people like trying to help me out like, "yo, get you into community college, ROTC," but once I got out, it was like, I stuck with it for a little while and I just went back to what I normally do, which was sell drugs, carry guns, because the environment that I lived in. I was kind of dumb. It wasn't like I needed to be out here selling drugs or whatever, but it was a time where I didn't have certain things that I wanted. I wasn't trying to get no job. I didn't even know how to do it. I was so young.

Shorty recognized the role of his environment (poverty and institutional racism) in contributing to his incarceration and unemployment, but he also subconsciously blamed himself for going to prison for several years between 1999 and 2012. By the time we met, he had been released from jail, but his feelings of personal humiliation remained palpable. When he was relaying his experience of prison, his face grew distant again, like on the day we met at the basketball park. He glanced downward. His voice trailed off. He did not finish sentences. He could not express his pain in words so he pointed toward the back of his head.[11] He touched his skull with his finger as he struggled to talk, and for some reason his gesture made my stomach hurt: "Being locked up, it took a piece of my mind, like it did something, like I ain't come out like I'm great. I don't know how to explain it. Like it took a piece of my mind like it's almost like, like, it kind of made me look bad . . ." His voice trailed off again. This was the absent presence behind Shorty's eyes that I felt haunted by earlier on the playground. It was eerie in its ability to escape words. He kept pointing toward the back of his head as if trying to touch an invisible wound. He had been hurt in a psychological sense, in prison, but there was a spectral dimension to his sense of injury that was hard to name.

As I thought about Shorty's invisible wound, it reminded me of a dream I had while conducting research for this book. I had fallen asleep while sitting in my dormitory room at Boston University. In the dream I had been born again and again, each time as a black man from a previous generation. But every time that I grew to maturity there was a white man standing there to murder me. So I kept dying, one black person after another, so many selves, all distorted through the mirror of history—always at the mercy of the other. Then finally, piercing the veil of time, I suddenly arrived face to face with myself, standing there in its nakedness. This self was something inconceivable to the other. In the act of dying and being reborn, I had been making jest of him all along. He could not kill me at last. I awoke, startled. I felt thankful to have witnessed something that the other could not misappropriate.

Watching Shorty's sullen face, I wondered if he would ever wake up from his living nightmare. His mind, body, and spirit seemed to bear the toll of living in a poverty-stricken and racialized world. He struggled to tell me that his beloved grandmother and his close friend Kane had both died while he was in prison. Shorty had been prohibited from attending their funerals, so their deaths represented a double loss. They were gone, but he was unable to see them into the next world. Shorty explained that the day I spotted him on the asphalt he was there to finally mourn Kane. Immediately following his release from prison, he went to the court to release his sorrow for Kane through his jump shot:

> I only came up to the park just for him. That's the only reason why I play. You know what I'm saying, that's the only reason why I said I was playing. I said, yo, you know, because he died when I was locked up so I was like yo, when I come home this summer, I'm balling. I ball for him, you know, he would have

wanted it. So that's why I came up there and balled. You know, I don't, you don't normally see me at the park.

So I did that on the strength for him, man, because we all was nice. He was watching me. I came out, hit a three, first shot of the day, hit a three, then hit a two like, he had me, he was holding me down, like go ahead, and we only played a half. I could see myself. I was about to get real loose. I was about to. I was amped.

Shorty recognized the movement of his body, the turn of the ball through the net, and the orderly succession of plays as signs of a reunion with Kane on the asphalt. In the process of remembering Kane, Shorty began feeling alive again, "loose" and "amped." His inclination to use the basketball court as a place of mourning caused me to reconsider the standard view in the literature, which says that "hoop dreams" are primarily motivated by status and social mobility. After our conversation, I never saw Shorty again on the asphalt. There are still days when I wonder if he has returned to some darkened penitentiary or, worse yet, joined other black ghosts, dead and unseen, haunting Boston's inner city landscapes. Toward the end of our conversation I looked down at Shorty's body and pointed to the black ink drawn across his leg: "Why do you have the letters 'LOL' tattooed on your leg?" I asked. Shorty looked at me and then down at his flesh: "It means Last Ones Left," he remarked. Shorty literally embodied the injury of exile, left behind in one of America's greatest cities.[12]

HOW DID WE GET HERE?
RELIGION, BASKETBALL, AND RACE

Boston's inner-city basketball courts are a repository for the suffering of its black communities. But how did we get here? How is it possible that a white minister from Canada invented a game capable of serving the existential needs of black youths toiling under racial and economic oppression? Remarkably, at its inception, basketball was conceived as a practice motivated by religion, though one geared for white men, who were battling against the moral and physical challenges of American urbanization. Nevertheless, black churches and organizations eventually adopted the sport, layering its religious dimensions with a critical cultural perspective.

Muscular Christianity and the Invention of Basketball

The convergence of religion, health, and sports in the late nineteenth and early twentieth centuries played a central role in Dr. James Naismith's invention of basketball in 1891. A Presbyterian minister and physical education specialist born in Ontario in 1861, Naismith found himself at the center of powerful changes in American religious ideology, economic life, and cultural attitudes toward the body, race, and masculinity. In the autumn of 1890 Naismith enrolled in the Young Men's Christian Association (YMCA) Training College in Springfield, Massachusetts, in order to realize "other effective ways of doing good besides preaching."[13]

Springfield's YMCA Training College was part of an American Christian movement dedicated to addressing the moral and physical dangers associated with the industrial revolution. "Muscular Christianity," as the movement was known, regarded physical health as a vital component of spiritual well-being—and this theological tenet became one of the central underpinnings for a Christian athletic response to urban decay. Rejecting Puritan concerns over the body's capacity to corrupt the soul, muscular Christians viewed physical prowess as an expression of God's glory. Following his senior year at McGill Theological Seminary, Naismith quit formal ministry and transferred to the YMCA Training College, becoming immersed in the new movement.

The historian William J. Baker suggests that muscular Christianity was also a response to the "feminizing tendencies" of the church and fragile notions of white masculinity in nineteenth-century America. As white women became more prominent in middle-class society and the church, white men laboring in urban factories could no longer define their manhood based on outmoded western frontier narratives. Muscular Christianity's convergence with athletics paved the way for urban white men to remain manly while staying connected to the church: "amidst the complexities of urban life, and during the last quarter of the century another kind of male dominance, athletic prowess, became a central feature in the definition of manliness. In North America, much more than in Britain, the YMCA played a crucial role in that transformation."[14]

Unfortunately, however, the YMCA and early proponents of muscular Christianity discouraged black Americans from participating in the new physical-culture movement. As blacks migrated en masse to Northern cities to escape the terror of Jim Crow in the early 1900s, they also discovered that the YMCA's mission to "develop 'the whole man—body, mind and spirit'"[15] did not apply to them. Although YMCA leaders advocated a Christian brotherhood fully committed to exercising the human body as God's temple, they simply did not recognize black people as full persons. YMCA leaders often subscribed to America's antiblack policies, proposing that blacks should be "separate but equal" within the organization. Although no evidence exists that Naismith himself excluded blacks, basketball's early association with the YMCA implied that the game was solely for the edification of white souls.

Racial Uplift Through Bodily Exercise

Despite separate-but-equal status within the muscular Christianity movement and the YMCA, black Americans enthusiastically formed their own physical-culture clubs with the express intent to use bodily exercise to empower the race. While many white men adopted muscular Christianity to cement their status above lower classes, blacks turned to physical culture to assert their humanity and to attain racial equality.[16] Despite meager finances and very little recreational space, blacks eventually established their own clubs so that "by the early twentieth century they had created a virtually autonomous African American YMCA."[17]

The Alpha Physical Culture Club of Harlem became arguably the most influential organization to transform Naismith's game into a black cultural art form of spiritual and political resistance in early-twentieth-century America. This section is greatly indebted to the research of historian Claude Johnson, who notes, "Jamaican-born brothers Gerald, Conrad, and Clifton Norman . . . founded the Alpha P.C.C. in 1904. Their establishment of the club made the Norman brothers the forerunners among blacks of what was then the brand new physical fitness movement. They were also at the root of the early evolution of basketball among people of color in the United States."[18]

The Norman brothers were distressed by the exclusion of blacks from muscular Christianity and the YMCA's recreational facilities. Conrad Norman stated in exasperation: "Although there were seventy thousand colored people in New York at the time, and the big city fairly teemed with athletic clubs of all kinds . . . there was not a single one devoted to colored people." However, due to their education and disciplined upbringing in Kingston, Jamaica, the Normans understood the vital connections between exercise, physical health, and well-being, particularly for an oppressed people. By 1904 they developed a program to educate the race on the merits of physical exercise as a means of survival and liberation. Conrad defined the mission: "We were helping our race by fortifying the bodies of our people in this, the struggle for existence, where only the fittest survive."[19]

Black churches were instrumental in fostering the mission of the Alpha P.C.C. through the new game of basketball. The Alpha P.C.C. began its operations in a "church house on West 134th Street in Harlem" and stood on the same street as St. Philip's Protestant Episcopal Church, "at that time . . . perhaps the most prestigious African-American church in the country." Father Everart Daniel, the newly appointed assistant minister of St. Philip's, was a close friend of the Normans and shared their mission to utilize sports as a buffer for black youths challenged by the dehumanizing effects of a racially divided city. Father Daniel borrowed from the Alpha P.C.C. model and turned St. Philip's community ministry program—then a bible-study group for young black men called the St. Christopher's Club—into "one of the most powerful forces in African-American athletics." The Alpha P.C.C. and St. Christopher's Club, along with two other black athletic clubs, the Smart Set Club and the Marathon Athletic Club of Brooklyn (affiliated with St. Augustine Protestant Episcopal Church, another black congregation), created the first organized black basketball teams in the country within a few years of each other. These four clubs—except for the Alpha P.C.C., which played the following year—participated in one of the first ever formally organized basketball tournaments between black teams, in 1907.[20]

Soon other black churches followed suit and formed their own basketball teams, such as the St. Cyprian Athletic Club, which was "the sports arm of the newly established St. Cyprian Episcopal Church," in 1908. The pastor's son, the star of the team, became Columbia University's first black basketball player and later the pastor of St. Martin's Episcopal Church in Harlem. Describing the dissemination of basketball throughout the black community in religious terms, Claude Johnson suggests that black churches "helped spread the 'gospel' of basketball further among African-Americans, particularly among West Indians."[21] From the beginning, black churches and clubs fused a religious ethos of ultimate worth and community uplift into the game.

In addition to the blessings of the black church, the visibility of black players' bodies as they moved across the court accounted for the rising popularity of the game. According to Johnson, the Alpha P.C.C. basketball team (also referred to as the "Alpha Big Five") attracted close to 1,200 fans per game in 1910, largely because players on the court embodied the aspirations of the community: Fans often identified with their neighborhood teams; players' abilities were viewed as heroic feats of character and moral virtue; women attended games in large numbers, and players entertained them during and after games; games generated significant amounts of money for those involved; and black basketball contests were seen as representations of racial achievement. Johnson expounds on this final point: "Since they felt that the club's success was also the race's success, the bigger picture was always kept in mind. When the Alpha Big Five played basketball it was about much more than just the game—it was about community building and racial self-esteem. The young club—as well as the athletic competition in general and the game itself—began to be seen as providing African Americans not only with an easily understood model for how to face challenges, but also with a source of inspiration and pride."[22] In this sense, basketball emerged within the black community as a stylized cultural model of spiritual and political transcendence.

As the black basketball subculture gained notoriety across the country so did the desire to capitalize on the commercial potential of the game. Bob Douglass, another Caribbean visionary and astute businessman, fought to organize the first black-owned all-black professional basketball team in the United States in 1923: the New York Harlem Renaissance Big Five (otherwise known as the "Harlem Rens"). Douglass realized before others that economic interests would have a profound impact on the game's evolution. He also believed that black basketball teams had to organize themselves professionally to compete against the best white teams in the country.

Douglass's grand vision for a professional black basketball team coincided with the explosion of black expressive culture during the Harlem Renaissance. The Harlem Rens' home floor, the Old

Renaissance Ballroom on 138th Street and Seventh Avenue, symbolized a synergy of black art forms in sports, music, and dance.[23] In this singular space, jazz musicians, dancers, and basketball players took the floor on the same night, expressing a shared desire for freedom through call and response, improvisation, and rhythmic beats. First, the Harlem Rens raced and spun across the floor and flew through the air to the rhythm of the ball against the hardwood. Then the hoops were removed and bands swung to complex layers of jazz notes as dancers shook waists, jumped over shoulders, and clapped hands throughout the night. In Kareem Abdul-Jabbar's documentary *On the Shoulders of Giants*, William Rhoden describes the activities at the Old Renaissance Ballroom: "I thought it was so cool because it just represented such a confluence of black culture, this confluence of dance and athleticism. All of it right there in that one building." For many, these performances served to encourage spiritual connections among blacks in ways similar to Sunday worship ceremonies. The son of Harlem Rens' star player, John Isaacs, described the spiritual ligature produced through the games: "It's like asking what did the Black Church mean to Harlem, its connection."[24]

The Rens' rootedness within the black community inspired the team to endure hardships on behalf of the race. From 1922 and well into the 1940s, the Rens "barnstormed" across the country, playing games against all-white teams, even in the South. They played almost 130 games a year to make a living, traveling long distances between contests due to the paucity of integrated hotels. They were verbally and physically assaulted by white onlookers and referees; scorekeepers cheated for the opposing side. Nevertheless, the Harlem Rens continued to sacrifice their bodies between the lines because they viewed each victory as an indictment of white supremacy.

Black ballplayers' efforts to topple white supremacy had gained momentum by 1939, when Chicago hosted the first ever World Professional Basketball Tournament. The Harlem Rens and Harlem Globetrotters (the other famous black professional team during this period) were both invited to participate.[25] When the Harlem Rens won the tournament, competing against the best white professional teams in the country (the Harlem Globetrotters won the following year), it was an important symbolic victory. The Rens' victory paved the way for William "Pop" Gates, one of the team's stars, to integrate the National Basketball League in 1946, a year before Jackie Robinson made his Major League Baseball debut.[26] Kareem Abdul-Jabbar refers to the Harlem Rens as "the greatest basketball team you never heard of" because of their unmatched influence on the game but relative erasure from the history of sports in the United States.[27]

THE UNDERSIDE OF VICTORY AND THE EMERGENCE OF STREET BASKETBALL IN U.S. CITIES

The integration of college basketball and the NBA was part of a larger struggle for civil rights in mid-twentieth-century America. Black Americans experienced unprecedented successes in the struggle for justice and equality, and black athletes played a significant role in the civil rights movement. Nevertheless, their achievements also resulted in unintended consequences for blacks at the bottom of the social ladder. As the civil rights movement came to an end and the black middle class expanded, opportunities and access for poor and working-class blacks actually declined. NAACP president Benjamin Jealous has put the problem succinctly: "We got what we fought for, but we lost what we had."[28]

The sociologist William Julius Wilson offers a compelling explanation for the rise of a black underclass in the United States following the civil rights movement. Wilson suggests that the persistence of historical patterns of racial discrimination, major economic changes, and demographic shifts have produced black inner-city neighborhoods "plagued by massive joblessness, flagrant and open lawlessness, and low-achieving schools. . . . Consequently, the residents of these areas . . . have become increasingly socially isolated from mainstream patterns of behavior."[29] These changes fostered an absence of middle-class role models and values in communities where there was once visionary leadership and a shared ethos of racial uplift. Today "the streets"—an alternative set of role models, institutions, and values that arose out of this vacuum—have become one of the primary contexts in which black youths are socialized in U.S. cities.[30] As one black athlete explained to me during an interview: "We were raised by the streets."

Holcombe Rucker and the Rise of Street Basketball

Within this emerging context of black urban exile, street basketball began to develop as a major cultural force among black youth. Just as black basketball fused with Harlem Renaissance jazz, dance, and civil rights in early- and mid-twentieth-century America, street basketball grew out of an "in your face" ethos of a young hip-hop generation increasingly frustrated with urban decay and social abandonment. The playground became a new locus for the convergence of black expressive culture in hip-hop, with rap music, break dancing, and a "go hard or go home" style of basketball often performed simultaneously on the same court. (One example of this confluence is DJ Cool Herc, one of the founders of rap music, who earned his nickname "Hercules" from his rough style of play on the basketball court.)[31] Although street ballers embodied the previous generation's belief that basketball was more than just a game—it was a mode of resistance—they did so within a new context of unprecedented street violence and the collapse of black social and institutional buffers (church, school, family, and so on).

Holcombe Rucker, a black World War II veteran and recreational parks director in New York City, set the spiritual tone and political agenda for the game on the playground. Following in the tradition of his athletic ancestors, he attempted to hold his first tournament in the late 1940s in St. Phillip's Church, which doubled as a community center. Stories abound regarding Rucker's passion for instilling discipline, love, and hope in players who faced police brutality, broken homes, and street violence. Vincent Mallozzi's oral history of the Rucker Tournament chronicles Rucker's ability to influence disinherited black men, such as the time he cried in front of his adolescent athletes to offer them a different model of masculinity and respect. One of his former players reflected on that moment with Rucker: "We were all tough kids from the streets. We had never seen a grown man cry before.... It was a lesson in discipline and respect that we would never forget."[32]

As the Black Fives era of segregated basketball teams came to an end in 1946, Rucker began organizing one of the first street-basketball tournaments in the country, between Lenox and Fifth Avenues on 138th Street. Rucker designed tournaments with little money, actually borrowing equipment from tournament players. Moreover, like his predecessors in the physical-culture movement, Rucker barnstormed with his teams across New York City, competing against Irish and Italian players and anyone else who would play them. Rucker moved his tournament to 128th Street and Seventh Avenue, at the St. Nicholas Houses playground, in 1949. Ingeniously, he expanded the tournament to include a professional division in 1954. By including pro players, Rucker turned his tournament and playground (which moved again to 130th Street and Seventh Avenue) into what became known as the "Mecca" of street basketball—a hallowed ground where basketball pilgrims trek to solidify their place in the annals of the game. Before moving the tournament to its current location at 155th Street and Eighth Avenue, Rucker began matching black professionals against street ballers in competitive play, showcasing legendary talents such as Wilt Chamberlain, "Dr." Julius Erving, Joe "Helicopter" Hammond, and Pee Wee Kirkland.

PEE WEE KIRKLAND, STREET VIOLENCE,
AND THE SPIRITUAL ESSENCE
OF STREET BASKETBALL

Pee Wee Kirkland's rise to legendary status in Harlem's street-basketball scene in the late 1960s and 1970s speaks volumes about basketball's changing role in the black struggle for dignity and place in the aftermath of the civil rights movement. A story that reads like an earlier edition of Shorty's, Kirkland's journey underscores the significance of playground basketball as mode of release and transcendence in the streets. Kirkland acknowledges that his role models did not consist of educated black visionaries such as the Norman brothers, Bob Douglass, or even Holcombe Rucker. His world was dominated by other figures and personalities commonly associated with today's inner cities: hustlers, gangsters, pimps, drug dealers, rappers, and athletes. These men and the terror of the streets they occupied shaped the context in which he played basketball at Rucker Park. Kirkland explains: "I remember being at Rucker and girls that I would have had towels and, under the towels, had sawed off shotguns. I mean it was real, the way Pee Wee Kirkland lived, 'cause I lived a double life. So when I left Rucker, I went to another world, the world of crime, the world of survival. It wasn't about basketball." Rucker Park in this sense, represented two opposing poles of Kirkland's identity—at once a refuge and a site of violence.

> I'd come to Rucker, after staying up all night long, and still have to score 30, 40 points. But when I got to Rucker, for that moment and that time in my life I was able to forget the life of crime. I was able to forget the streets. I was able to forget the drugs. I was able to forget everything for that particular time in my life. It was like magic.

Kirkland suggests that only God could design a place like Rucker Park, which exposed black men's greatness in the sludge of urban degradation: "It's God that designed that. That ain't man's design. Rucker is a place that God designed to expose greatness."

It wasn't corporate, it was real, man, and it's something I love. Man, I wouldn't be alive today if wasn't for street basketball. That's how guys saw it back then. It was in your blood. You felt it. It was in your spirit. It wasn't just a paycheck. It was for real, man. It was in your heart and in your soul and that's the essence of street basketball, man.[33]

Kirkland's devotion to street basketball as a physical exercise, which saved his spirit, is certainly in line with Naismith's original vision for hoops. However, when Naismith invented the game, he could not have imagined downtrodden black males dancing on the asphalt to establish an ultimate connection with themselves and the universe. Yet Kirkland reports that sometimes his interaction with the crowd of black onlookers and his intense focus on the game would take him to an-Other time, beyond his current difficulties:

The crowd would just take me there. I remember one time I was on a fast break and I was fixin' to throw it down, but my mind was so obsessed with the crowd and wanting to rock the crowd I ended up going behind the pole coming back to the foul line, just re-rocking again and went and when I went to the basket instead of laying it up I flipped the ball like this here under my arm like that and a guy named Larry Cheetah grabbed it, hit it on the backboard twice and then dunked it. The crowd stood up. That's what I'm saying about Rucker. It's essentially a show time, but we took show time to another time.[34]

Kirkland's double life in the streets eventually led to the forfeiture of an NBA contract with the Chicago Bulls and several years of incarceration. Nevertheless, it would be a mistake to overlook the role of basketball in Kirkland's life as a source of meaning, stability, and spirit, which fosters his "continued struggle for a more liberated existence."[35]

Basketball emerged in late-nineteenth-century America as a white male Christian response to the industrial revolution. Its inventor, James Naismith, recognized the value of physical exercise as a mode of mental catharsis and spiritual edification, which countered the effects of city life. However, black Americans migrating to Northern cities to escape Jim Crow segregation were turned away from the recreational facilities of the YMCA. Black pioneers in exercise responded by forming their own physical-culture clubs with the support and blessings of black churches. Shortly thereafter, the black community transformed the game of basketball into a stylized expression of spiritual and cultural transcendence that shared similarities with jazz music and Lindy Hop dance. This basketball subculture exploded onto the national scene in the 1940s due to the dogged efforts of all-black teams such as the Alpha Big Five, Harlem Rens, and Harlem Globetrotters. Black athletes could not longer be excluded from national basketball leagues.

In the wake of American integration in sports and other social arenas, however, a sharp class and intergenerational divide emerged within the black community. As the black middle class vacated inner cities, economic opportunities for poor and working-class African Americans also declined. At the same time, the black church, black family, and other institutional buffers that had served to mitigate the effects of persistent racial discrimination began to deteriorate in urban communities. The streets filled this vacuum, emerging as one of the primary socializing institutions of black inner-city youth. Street basketball (in addition to rap music, break dancing, etc.) rose up as

an athletic response to social abandonment and urban violence, especially among black males, who began to view the basketball court as
a refuge from the cruelty of the city. Although predominately white
corporate interests have attempted to turn their stylized expressions
of struggle into products of economic consumption, playground
basketball remains a vital source of feeling and meaning for black
youth living in urban exile, which it remains for those playing in Boston's contemporary inner-city basketball world.

2

BOSTON'S MEMORIAL GAMES

From 2010 through 2014 I spent time on the asphalt with African American ballplayers in Boston's inner-city neighborhoods in order to research the forms of experience street basketball affords. This approach gave me access to the lived experiences of these black youths, a dimension scholars often overlook.

My personal background as a Roxbury native and former street-ball player also made it easier to avoid reducing players' bodies to objects determined by fixed cultural narratives. While I did not ignore the cultural forces at play in my analysis, I became acutely aware of the ache for meaning and feeling expressed in the games. In this sense, our shared social proximity helped me to avoid stripping these young black men of their agency.

I collected data in the form of field notes. Field notes consist of an ethnographer's ongoing observations, experiences, and feelings over the course of research. They are similar to diary entries and are usually written before, during, and after time in the field. I generally wrote field notes during and after street-basketball tournaments or immediately following an important conversation in the neighborhood. Whenever possible, I attempted to reproduce conversations with subjects verbatim and to jot down notes soon after an incident occurred. The process of writing field notes is central to ethnography since it involves ongoing data collection and analysis.

During the production of field notes, researchers begin defining units of meaning pertinent to research questions. Over the course of an ethnographic project, these units of meaning can be compared to other units as the researcher builds a fuller account of the phenomenon under consideration. In many cases, as new meanings appear, the researcher is provoked to consider a new point of view and to seek more information. This occurred early in my fieldwork when one ballplayer told me that he went to the basketball court to "let it all out"—to release pain. His comments made me reconsider standard views about hoop dreams. Once the ethnographer reaches the "saturation point" where no new data can be reasonably collected and coded for meaning, the final step is to write up the research. The process of writing is another mode of analysis that involves comparing data with previous conclusions in the literature and arriving at potentially new insights.

In addition to ethnography and participant observation, I conducted in-depth interviews with several ballplayers. I chose young men between the ages of eighteen and thirty-nine who were part of Boston's street-basketball community. I was struck by the emotional intensity of the interviews. Bourdieu suggested that marginalized individuals might experience a field interview as an exceptional opportunity to speak freely from the usual constraints of an oppressive world. He maintained that an interview, which is "freed from the usual constraints (particularly of time) that weigh on most everyday interchanges . . . helps create the conditions for an extra-ordinary discourse, which might have never been spoken, but which was already there, merely waiting for the conditions of its actualization."[1] For many of the black athletes, our interview was the first time someone had expressed genuine interest in their stories. Momentarily freed from the burden of the streets, they shared experiences and feelings that may have remained silenced. Our interviews became an opportunity for "self-examination . . . simultaneously gratifying and painful . . . to give vent, at times with an extraordinary *expressive intensity*, to experiences and thoughts long kept unsaid or repressed."[2]

In addition, I viewed and studied documentaries on basketball in the United States in general and street basketball in particular. I used these secondary sources to validate themes that arose from field notes and interviews. The visual aspects of these films offered another medium to observe basketball players in motion while simultaneously expanding my coverage of the game to include more than just the communities I directly observed.

THE SETTING: BOSTON INNER-CITY HOOPS

Three predominately black neighborhoods make up the heart of Boston's inner-city community. These neighborhoods—Roxbury, Dorchester, and Mattapan—are adjacent geographically and contain myriad side streets and corners, government housing projects, churches, high schools, liquor stores, community centers, and basketball courts that spill across the urban landscape. To the black youth living in these neighborhoods, especially the young men, community centers, street corners, and basketball courts are prominent socializing spaces. These places are central to the institution of the "streets," where, in addition to schools, churches, mosques, and so forth, these young men spend considerable time constructing their identities.

As a socializing institution, Boston's streets are organized around a complex set of identity options and communal spaces where young black men spend time together. One of the most prominent identity options for young black men within the neighborhoods is gang membership. Gangs often claim specific corners, avenues, and housing projects as territory. Young men rep their street-gang affiliations by standing on particular corners, sitting on stoops, and wearing gang insignia, thereby constituting a highly visible form of black masculinity in the neighborhood. In fact, for many of Boston's black youth, gangs are synonymous with particular neighborhoods and streets. The gangs of Boston's black neighborhoods do not use signifiers such as Crips or Bloods to identify themselves. Rather, most gangs take their names from the housing project or street in which their members actually live. For example, Copeland Street, which is the name of a recognizable street in Roxbury, is also the moniker for its gang. In this sense, if there is a political geography of Boston's inner city among black youth, gang members are its most prominent stakeholders.

The dominant presence and power of gangs in the streets may also be seen in the assumptions black youth make regarding gang membership and affiliation. In many cases, for a young black man to be born and raised in a particular housing project or avenue implies his affiliation with the gang controlling that area. Even if he shuns affiliation, he remains marked as a member of his neighborhood gang by youth in adjacent neighborhoods. Baron, a street-ball player who became one of my main informants, explained:

> Well I mean, growing up living in Boston you had a lot of different gangs and you had to pretty much protect where you came from. Even if you didn't have to, someone made you because I lived in the James Street Projects them years. Most of my family and my friends are all from the projects. So, James Street at the time was one of the notorious gangs in Boston, the biggest projects in Boston, and everybody knew it. So wherever I would go, I never represented James Street. I never went to places like "yeah, I'm from the James Street." It would just be like "okay, I seen him with some James Street kids. Let's ask him if he's from James Street." And my whole attitude was "yeah, I'm from James Street but I don't have nothing to do with whatever they do with y'all." But if you ask me again, now I know what you really want. Now I'm starting to swing. Now I'm getting aggravated. I want to get it on. That pretty much made me a fighter.

Gangs, in this sense, occupy a structural position in the streets in the socialization of many black youth. This partially explains why gang affiliation is felt to be a forced identity marker for some of Boston's young black men. Many spoke as if they could not avoid the influence of gangs. Rather, gangs were often taken for granted as a natural part of social reality. This observation should give pause to those who assume gang membership or affiliation is always by choice.

One exception to this normative structure is granted to Boston's street-basketball players. Gang members who control specific neighborhoods often grant ballplayers a "pass" from illicit activities. If a ballplayer becomes well known across the city, rival gangs will also show him respect and offer him relatively safe passage in the streets. As symbols of hope, ballplayers garner devotion and respect. Jermaine, a street-ball player from Roxbury, explained how his game protected him from the gangs:

> One of the gangs was right behind my house. It was Avon Street Homes and it was right behind my house. Dealing with it, I tried my best to stay away from it, but it's tough when you go to the park in the summertime and they are there and we are playing basketball. So you get to know the people in your neighborhood that are gang members and are this. And for the most part, that's what they do and they were fine with me. I didn't have problems. I didn't have too many of those obstacles because that round ball, man. Basketball is a platform in the avenue to get you from anywhere. I don't care whatever is going on, if you can do this, whatever your struggle is people will tend to leave you alone a little bit. Because you form some kind of a bond, and that is what I use as my catapult to keep the gang members off of me or trying to recruit me. They just saw that I could play a little ball so they gave me a little pass.

The collective assumption that ballplayers are predestined for greatness sets them apart from their wider communities. In this sense, street-ball players embody what the sociologist of religion Émile Durkheim referred to as the sacred, that which is "set apart" and distinct from the profanity of everyday life.[3] As I mentioned, monikers bestowed on black street-ball players, such as black Jesus, indicate their communities' adoration of street ballers as saviors.

Clearly however, the distinction between ballplayers and gang members, the sacred and the profane, is an artificial one, which is often transgressed by young men performing both roles simultaneously. As Jermaine acknowledged, street-basketball courts are generally located within gang territories. Ballplayers and gang members socialize in the same spaces and develop deep bonds. In addition, some of Boston's street-basketball courts are closed to outsiders. In order to step on the court safely, one has to have an affiliation with the gang in that area or be so well "known" that even rival gang members will show you love. To venture onto a court without tacit permission from gang members residing there is not streetwise.

Of course, there are other identity options for Boston's inner-city young black men that fall outside the scope of this book (such as an artist or a student). However, the majority of the young men I interviewed seemed to believe that being a gang member, athlete, or music artist, were their only options.

In addition to street basketball, community centers play an important role in supporting the aspirations of ballplayers in Boston. During the winter months, basketball moves indoors, and these spaces provide an additional outlet for young men to hone their skills while keeping some distance from the gangs. Community centers are important socializing spaces because they give ballplayers— some of whom are fatherless—access to caring adults and role models who do not subscribe to the illicit values of the streets. One community center in particular, now referred to as the Yawkey Club of

Roxbury, became an epicenter for city hoops in the heart of Boston's black community.

The Yawkey Club was the organizational hub for the legendary Boston Shootout Tournaments of the 1990s. The Boston Shootout was a nationally recognized high school basketball tournament, second in reputation and quality of play only to the McDonald's All-American game. Major U.S. cities, including New York, Washington, D.C., Philadelphia, Atlanta, Los Angeles, Detroit, and Boston, participated each year, sending one team of their best high school basketball players to compete in games over three days. As a child, I remember sitting in New York City's team locker room, staring at future Knicks point guard Stephon Marbury as he leaned back against metal lockers, arms crossed, listening to his coach at halftime. A few minutes later, he stepped onto the court and caught an alley-oop dunk in the middle of the lane that sent the crowd into a frenzy. During another game I sat underneath the basket enthralled as "The Truth," Paul Pierce, dribbled the ball to the right baseline and took off like a "bird in flight."[4] He was so high that his head nearly hit the backboard. Pierce finally glided to the left side of the hoop and flipped the ball off the glass, scoring two points for his Los Angeles squad. Pierce was passionate. He screamed "ahhhhh!" in midair as the ball swished through the net and fell to the hardwood. I also loved watching Boston's teams, which always included neighborhood stars whom I recognized from the playgrounds and local gyms. One year, I was able to witness Wayne Turner carry our Boston team all the way to the finals. A few years later, Turner led the University of Kentucky Wildcats to two national titles before signing a contract with the Boston Celtics and Harlem Globetrotters. I enjoyed watching Turner play on national television, especially since I got to shoot around with him at the Yawkey Club one quiet Saturday morning as a young man. Boston city basketball legends such as Patrick Ewing, Dana Barros, Jamal Jackson,

Monty Mack, Jonathan DePina, Shannon Crooks, and Courtney Eldridge all played in the Boston Shootout games.

Although the Boston Shootout has fallen apart in recent years due to waning sponsorship, the Yawkey Club still plays an important role in the hoop dreams of Boston's young black men. For this reason, and because of my local ties to the club, I decided to return to the center as one of my first stops when I began to study Boston city hoops. When I walked through the main doors, the elderly mother of my youth basketball coach, Manny Wilson, greeted me at the counter. "Onaje, is that you?! Hey baby! Where you been? It's been so long. Look at you. You look so handsome! Come here and give me a hug!" Ms. Wilson beamed with joy. I reached behind the counter to give Ms. Wilson a big hug. "Hi Ms. Wilson. How have you been Mom?" I asked. "These kids are crazy nowadays boy," she responded. "Ain't like when y'all was growing up. They don't listen to nobody, killing each other out here. But I'm glad you're back my son. They need to see young men like you. By the way, I'd like you to coach one of the teams in my son's memorial league, the Manny Wilson Basketball League. Manny would be so proud of you boy!" she remarked. "Thanks Mom," I responded softly, as I thought about her son, the father figure I fell in love with as a child, whose chest was crushed in a car accident at a Roxbury intersection.

I was on a public bus, riding past Roxbury Community College, when I saw Manny's mangled police car wrapped around a curbside pole. As soon as I got home, I received a call from my friend "Tee": "Manny is gone, man. He's gone!" Tee was crying. I was twelve years old and could not understand the meaning of death. Manny was a Boston Police officer, a basketball coach, and a father figure to countless kids in our neighborhood. I was Manny's "favorite" in addition to another boy he nicknamed "Scud Webb" because his jump shot looked like an errant missile careening toward the hoop. Manny took us on rides in his car after Saturday basketball practice, and if there was a hoops skills clinic in the area, he always made sure

I was there to learn. He played games with us too, like any father would, chasing us down the street when we punched him in the leg and ran, and he brought us his favorite candy from the local store: Sugar Daddies. We loved Manny. He was our hero.

The day after the incident, I felt confused and all alone. I didn't really know how to grieve; all I felt was the pain in my heart. I knew that Manny was gone, but to where? No one discussed his death with me, so seeking answers I naturally went to go to the basketball court where Manny and I had shared so many warm memories. It was a Sunday morning, the day after his death, and the Yawkey Club was practically empty. Bobby, a janitor, who often referred to himself as a "poolologist" because he schooled all us kids in billiards, saw my saddened face through glass windows and let me through the locked doors. I felt disoriented when I stepped onto the court, as if the hardwood, the hoop, the ball, and my body were floating in a mass of confusion, unhinged from the ordinary laws of gravity. I dribbled and shot the ball toward the basket, but nothing seemed to move quite right. A question kept hovering around my head: where is Manny? My head began feeling woozy, and my body was filled with a strange sadness as I dribbled and went for the double-pump lay-up Manny had once taught me. Breathing heavily, I walked over to the bleachers, sat down with the ball on my lap, and stared out into the open space of the court.

"Hi, can we talk for a moment?" a voice spoke from a distance. "Huh?" I said startled, looking over to the left, near the gym entrance. "I hear that you were one of Coach Manny Wilson's boys," a reporter from the *Boston Herald* said while approaching me. I nodded my head, holding on tightly to my basketball. "What did Manny mean to you? How important was he in your life?" the reporter asked. "Manny was the father that I never had," I responded, looking up at her face. A few years later my biological father would return and transform my life, but on that day, that was how I felt, all alone. Recently, I discovered the picture that the

Figure 2.1 Onaje Woodbine, 1992.
Source: Photo by Bill Belknap. Courtesy of the *Boston Herald*.

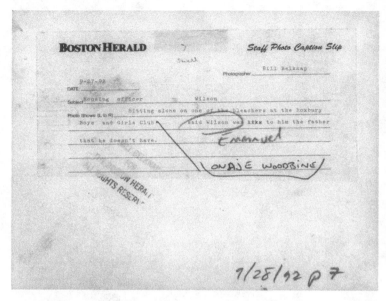

Figure 2.2 *Boston Herald* Caption Slip.
Source: Courtesy of the *Boston Herald*.

Boston Herald photographer took of me that day as I sat on the sidelines searching for Manny.

I was delighted to see Manny's mother at the Yawkey Club after all those years. "Mom, it would be an honor to coach in the Manny Wilson Basketball League," I told her. "Good baby," she said smiling. "I'll get you all the information now that I see you'll be around more. How's that Ph.D. program? Oh yes, I heard about it! Don't think I ain't been keeping tabs on you, doctor!" I couldn't stop smiling. She was like a grandmother to me, a loving elder who had watched me grow up, and she adored me. The love that resounded through her voice made me feel like I was the most valuable being in the world. "It's going good, Ma." I said. "I am doing research on the religious dimensions of basketball. That's part of the reason why I'm

Figure 2.3   Manny Wilson League Banner.
Source: Photo by author.

here." "Well, good, go up and check out the gym. The boys are probably up there right now," she pointed to the stairs. "Thanks Mom," I agreed. "I'll stop by to say goodbye before I leave." "Okay, boy," Ms. Wilson said, as she turned her attention to a few kids running down the hallway.

The gym seemed so much smaller now that I was older, but the walls and creaking hardwood contained memories that sent my imagination flying into the past. As I watched young men race up and down the court at the behest of an older coach barking instructions, I remembered being in their shoes. This was the same court where I had once grieved for Manny and honed my love for the game. I happened to look over toward the left and spotted a banner with Manny's image hanging from the walls. The sign read: "Manny Wilson Basketball League: Gone but not forgotten."

I decided to sit on the bleachers and watch the young boys play ball for a while. Their coach was schooling them in values of the game—teamwork, discipline, and self-respect—as they sprinted up and down the floor. As I observed him instruct his players, I was proud to be a part of this tradition but also very aware of how the community center imposes a particular narrative of hoop dreams on inner-city young men. Community-center counselors promote middle-class values of good sportsmanship and fair play, which gives the games a certain organized flavor. Moreover, there are many young men in the streets over whom they have no influence. Since I wanted access to the unscripted manner in which the game is played in the streets, I eventually decided to leave the Yawkey Club to experience the game in its most unregulated form. On the asphalt, the games are mainly organized by the players themselves. After spending a few more moments in the gym, I walked downstairs and spotted Ms. Wilson again. "Mom, I'll make sure to come back soon and thanks for inviting me to coach in the Manny Wilson League." "Okay, boy," she said. "And you be safe out there, you hear?" "Yes, Mom."

Gaining access to black Boston's street-basketball courts is difficult and at times dangerous. I needed an informant with the street credentials to "vouch" for me and keep me out of harm's way. I made a few phone calls and finally got in touch with an old childhood friend and fellow street-ball player named Baron, whom I had once nicknamed "the Body Guard" because of how he protected his teammates on the court. "B, I am doing this project on street basketball in Boston. I need your help." "Onaje, is that you?" he asked. "Yeah, it's me," I responded. "You got it. You know that you don't even have to ask," he explained, his voice full of base and confidence. "Thanks, B. I really appreciate it, man. When is the next tournament? I'll come see you play, if that's cool." "Yeah, man, no problem. Come down to the Save R Streets Basketball Classic on the hill near Memorial Middle School." "Cool, my brother. I'll see you there."

BARON: THE BODY GUARD

Baron, a six-foot-two-inch, 250-pound former fighter with piercing eyes, became both my teacher and protector in Boston's world of inner-city hoops. When we were growing up the Body Guard had a reputation for knocking people out with his fists. His role on our neighborhood basketball team was to be the protector. Whenever we played teams from other territories in Roxbury, Dorchester, or Mattapan, we felt safe after games because Baron knew almost every gang member in the crowd. In his thirties, Baron has given up fighting and focuses his energy on uniting Boston's black community through basketball. His success in reconciling rival gang members through basketball is mainly due to his personality and the "street cred" he earned as a child moving between foster homes. Each time he ran away from a new group home, Baron would have to walk several miles through gangland just to make it back to his mother's house in the projects. The police would be waiting for him when he arrived at his mother's, but it didn't matter to Baron. He just wanted to see his mother and take a break from the horrid conditions inside the crowded homes of social services. During those walks, Baron developed friendships with all types of gang members, even those from rival streets corners, and because he was fearless and could fight, he eventually earned respect from his peers. He also earned instant credibility in the streets after he survived being shot and stabbed multiple times. Baron is one of the few guys in Boston's black neighborhoods who has the ability to walk through almost any gang territory without fear.

When I arrived at the Save R Streets Basketball Classic I could hear the rhythmic thud of rap beats vibrating in the distance. Two asphalt courts stood side by side, and in between the beat were the sounds of sneakers scratching the pavement, ballplayers yelling "oooooutlet," basketballs clanging off rims, and onlookers screaming, "He can't guard you, he can't handle the truth!" Spectators were sitting on metal bleachers, hanging off stone walls, and standing around sidelines jawing with the players. Hidden behind the whole scene were gang members and hustlers, slightly out of view. The smell of marijuana wafted from behind the bushes where they huddled together, smoking and gambling. Baron was already on the court, playing for his team from Roxbury. As I moved closer toward the asphalt, a guy I did not recognize tapped my shoulder. "Damn, it's good to see a legend out here. Onaje, I ain't seen you in years. I like what I see," he said with a nod of approval as he moved passed me. I was always shocked by this community's capacity to remember its basketball stars. Stories of street-basketball players were passed down, and players' abilities were debated and ranked repeatedly. People I had never met personally would approach and acknowledge me as a ballplayer. The recognition I received from the stranger who tapped me on the shoulder comforted me, and I gathered the courage to nestle my way between bodies standing along the sidelines. Baron was barreling down the court with the ball in his hand, playing his signature style that was at once menacing and comedic. Nearly 250 pounds, he always wanted to be a point guard. As he brought the ball up the court, smaller players bounced off him like flies. "Stop reaching!" someone yelled in the crowd. Baron finally took the ball to the right block to post-up a smaller player underneath the basket. Sweat poured from his fat forehead as he huffed and puffed, trying to bully the poor guy on his back. Baron dipped his shoulder into his opponent's chest and bounced him backward onto the pavement. He missed the layup, but luckily the referee called a two-shot foul. As Baron stood on the free-throw line rubbing the ball between his hands, one dark-skinned young man on the sidelines who must have weighed as much as Baron, yelled out: "Baron, you're too slow to do anything out there!" Baron dribbled the ball and released the free throw into the air: "Yeah, and you're too fat to guard me!" Everyone busted out laughing as the shot splashed through the net.

When Baron was not playing ball, he was on the sidelines taking notice of the various gang members around the court. During tournaments there is often an implicit but fragile peace between gang members, and Baron always seemed to be monitoring the truce. Baron's dress and demeanor are generally conservative: black T-shirt and black pants, with his round head shaved bald. Standing with him in the intermediate circle of the court, I often received an education in the hidden rules of the park. "He's from Red Street gang, he shouldn't be over here by himself. He's risking his life right now. That guy right there, he is going to play ball at St. Jude's Prep. He's got a shot to play D One. See those two guys, they are from rival gangs, but they squashed [reconciled] it for the tournament. Yo, John, come and meet my boy Onaje. John, do you know who I just introduced you to right now?! This man, Onaje Woodbine, is a street-ball legend. If he had his sneakers on, he'd give you fifty [points] right now." John smiled at me as if to say, "Yeah, I'd like to see him try it." Baron is an intimidating presence, but his comedic side draws the admiration of everyone. Having him "vouch" for me as one of his boys during the course of my research assuaged any fears that I felt while approaching some players and gang members.[5] Without Baron's willingness to trust me and to explain the dynamics of the court, my attempt to examine the religious dimensions of Boston street basketball would not have succeeded.

While spending time with Baron, one of my most significant revelations regarding the "lived religion" of Boston street basketball was that nearly every single street-ball tournament is designed to memorialize black men who have died before their time. I kept a record of each tournament, their order of succession, and catalogued specific tournament themes.

MEMORIAL GAMES

Generally speaking, Boston's street-basketball tournaments are designed to address the most pressing concerns of this community—fatherlessness, violence, poverty, illness, and racism, but premature death is by far the most salient theme. The players themselves generally decide on the focus of each tournament. One of two exceptions to this is the Malcolm X League, which community organizers Rufus Faulk and David Lewis Jr. formed with the Boston TenPoint Coalition of black Christian ministers in 2011 to foster a "season of peace" in the community.[6] Drawing from a historical connection between basketball and the black church, the TenPoint Coalition chose Malcolm X Park for the site of the league. Malcolm X Park is considered the Mecca of Boston street basketball, largely because of its gang-neutral location. This means that ballplayers and crowds from different neighborhoods are free to congregate, socialize, and compete. Using hoops as their vehicle, the TenPoint Coalition attempted to forge a truce between the gangs at Malcolm X Park. Rufus explained to me that pastors and players opened the first game with a prayer, and players were encouraged to have informal conversations with pastors throughout the duration of the league. A symbol of a basketball with the letter "X" and the words "season of peace" hung from the fence surrounding the court and was imprinted on players' jerseys.

Another exception to player organization of neighborhood basketball is the Boston Neighborhood Basketball League, which is organized by the city and several community centers. BNBL is a citywide league, in which teams from each of Boston's black neighborhoods compete over the entire summer. Each team is organized by a local community center and coached by neighborhood elders. Eventually, two teams, from separate neighborhoods, emerge to compete in a championship game. Because BNBL involves many black youth in the city, it is popular, and each summer the championship team takes home special bragging rights for their neighborhood. At the same time, BNBL is organized from the top down by various clubhouses, YMCAs, and recreational centers and is more scripted than street-basketball tournaments.

Street-basketball tournaments are designed by the players themselves and take place during consecutive weekends throughout the summer. Since the location and date of each tournament is fairly stable from one summer to the next (sometimes old tournaments give way to new ones), Boston's street-basketball community moves from court to court within the flow of an unwritten calendar during the summer months. No matter what difficulties the young players face during the week, during the weekends they flock to the asphalt to reclaim their humanity. After attending a few tournaments with Baron and noticing that most of them were dedicated to people who had died prematurely, some violently, I asked Baron if he knew how many games were memorials to the dead. His response floored me: "Honestly, I can probably say all of them." Over several summers, I confirmed his observation. Below are the names and themes of each tournament in their proper order.

The Chill Will Tournament, also referred to as Chill's Diamond Ring Educational Foundation Basketball Tournament, is in early June and kicks off the summer street-ball games. Since it is held at Malcolm X Park, the best ballplayers attend. Willie "Chill" Veal, or "Chill Will," organizes this tournament in memory of his late son, Little Chill, who was murdered in the streets of Boston. He also dedicates the games to Paris Booker, a young man who was close to the family before he was fatally hit by a car while riding his bicycle. Chill Will organizes the tournament to empower city youth, especially with information regarding financial literacy, which they rarely receive in traditional classrooms or in the home. With the Diamond Ring Educational Foundation Basketball Tournament, Chill Will has attempted to bequeath a legacy of healing and entrepreneurship to his own children and those living in the neighborhoods. During one of our conversations, Chill explained: "Basketball is my release. My family knows that I have to play basketball every week and everything stops when I'm playing. That's how you let go of all your problems." Played in the shadow of Little Chill, the tournament is always intense, and because teams are organized by neighborhood, their affiliate gangs are often in attendance on the outer circle of the court. Although Chill Will's tournament is by far one of the most positive events of the summer, on rare occasions gang violence from the surrounding streets can spill onto the court. In June 2013, during a game that I was fortunate enough to miss, a young man drove by in his SUV and blasted eight gunshots into a crowd of onlookers. No one was hit, but the following day I was standing with several witnesses on the same bullet-riddled basketball court discussing the drive-by shooting. Many ballplayers I spoke with knew the person who fired the shots, but no one would say his name. They offered minimal details. He had been in a fight near the park a few minutes earlier and had lost. He drove by the court and sprayed bullets into the crowd with spite and anger. I was scared as they told the story, given that we were standing at the scene of the crime.

What really surprised me, however, was the casual nature of our conversation—the way the other ballplayers stood there discussing the shooting as if it had been normal. These young men seemed numbed to the violence. My behavior probably seemed strange to them as I glanced nervously around the court as if another shooting was imminent.

The Chill Will Tournament is followed by Dre's Tournament, played in the memory of Dre's late father, Emmanuel, just as the summer moves toward Father's day. As Baron explained, "Once Dre's Tournament starts, it goes all the way through the end of the summer." The Save R Streets Summer Classic follows Dre's Tournament. Three street-ball players and several others from Roxbury organize these games every year. They formed the tournament to curb inner-city violence and to encourage the development of talent in the neighborhood. In 2010, these young men decided to design a ritual to honor black youths who had been murdered in the streets. During one of their games, white doves, Christian symbols of peace for departed souls, were lofted into the air to remember youth who had died of violence. By acknowledging lives lost in the past, the organizers sought to generate hope in the future. They explained that ultimately they were attempting to celebrate life and a better tomorrow.

Figure 2.4 Chill Will Tournament Banner.
Source: Photo courtesy of Diamond Ring Tournament.

Three young organizers of the Save R Streets Summer Classic share a special bond through hoops. One summer afternoon during the middle of the week, I caught the three of them in a heated game of "twenty-one" at Malcolm X. Park. Twenty-one, sometimes referred to as "New York twenty-one," does not follow the rules of a regular basketball game because it is played on a half court without teams. Each individual competes against the rest. The games are rough and chaotic partly because there are no personal fouls, and rules against traveling, double-dribbling, or palming are nonexistent. This opposition to rules also gives twenty-one a creative edge because it encourages players' improvisational abilities. As I watched these three young men express their individuality while remaining supportive of each other under the hot sun, their joy in being together was obvious. That each wore the same style and color basketball shorts adorned with a

Figure 2.5 Save R Streets Banner.
Source: Courtesy of Score4More Inc.

shared logo seemed fitting. Save R Streets Summer Classic is a public expression of the bond basketball has created in their lives.

Following the Save R Streets Summer Classic is the Community Awareness Tournament organized by Russell Paulding. This tournament is held every summer in the memory of three deceased black youth—two of whom are Marvin Barros Jr. and Eric Paulding. Russell always leaves the third spot on the banner open in anticipation of a new murder victim each year. Similar to Carrie Mae Weems's photographic depiction of an "empty chair" inhabited by the spirit of the dead in her *Sea Island Series* (1992), Russell saves an empty place on the banner, until it is eventually occupied by the face of one of Boston's black and newly deceased.[7]

Marvin Barros Jr., who became a big brother to me through basketball, died at twenty-one due to complications from the blood disorder hemophilia. Before his death, everyone said that he had an "old soul," and he often mentored black youth, even though they were sometimes close in age. Marvin was six-foot-four-inches tall, skinnier than a telephone pole, dark-skinned, and four years older than me when I was a child. "Mom," I said one day when I was ten, showing up after school with Marvin by my side. "This is Marvin. He is my friend and he wants to stay the night. Is that okay?" "Uhhh, yeah, I guess it's okay, Onaje. Did he call his mother?" my mother asked, wondering what I was doing with a friend who was twice my size and a teenager. Since that day when we confused my mother, Marvin never left me. No one ever saw us apart. He would stay over at my mother's apartment for months at a time. When he was ready to leave, I would follow and spend the night at his parent's place for months. Marvin loved the game of basketball and because he touched so many young lives, the Yawkey Club named its teen center after him when he died.

Being around young people and basketball gave Marvin courage to deal with his crippling disease. He could hardly play the game himself because of his fragile joints, so he lived vicariously through us. From the sidelines, Marvin defied others' expectations, creating artwork and writing poems, especially about how God could use basketball to transform people's pain and suffering. When NBA star Earvin "Magic" Johnson was diagnosed with HIV Marvin felt a special kinship with Magic, who also faced a blood-borne illness that took him off the court. Especially moved, Marvin wrote a poem for Johnson entitled "Let it Be Magic," in which he recognized NBA stars as biblical prophets who were sent by God to empower humanity to overcome obstacles. For a fifteen-year-old boy from Roxbury, the poem was a sensitive exploration of the convergence of hoops, religion, and the human condition. Years later, after Marvin's death, Marvin's mother shared his poem with me and to my surprise, written on the page in Magic's own handwriting were the words: "Magic Johnson #32. I hope all your dreams come true." Magic Johnson had actually read his words and felt moved to send him a note. Marvin's mother supplied me with a copy of the original poem, which I have transcribed below.

LET IT BE MAGIC

In the beginning God brought us to
the center of the world when he
brought us the hustle of Big Bill
Russell.

He brought us a goliath of a man
When he named Wilt Chamberlain.
Who's rule brought order to the land
Who's rule brought order on the court.

God brought us to dream, a vision of
ways and means, his name reigns
supreme, life's shining star, his
name is Kareem Abdul Jabar.

He brought us "Moses," Moses Malone
Who towers as high as Mount Sinai.

The man who brought the ten commands
to the courts "promise land."

He created a bird,[8] one "Larry Bird"
who's message is to deliver the
deliverance for all to see and for
all to hear.

God brought us the prophet "Isaiah,"
Isaiah Thomas, a man of promise in a
big man's world to keep them honest.
A smile of pearls that rules both
worlds.

God brought us "Jordan," Michael
Jordan, like a river he flows
through every heart like a fine work
of modern art.

Then came the virus H.I.V. then came
the "plague" called AIDS. If we are
to [handle] this crusade we'd have
to add another disciple to the
bible, and let him be immortal, to
keep us all strong with the will to
go on.

Then "Let it be MAGIC"
Then "Let it be MAGIC"
So, God chose Earvin "super magic"
Johnson.

Marvin Barros Jr.

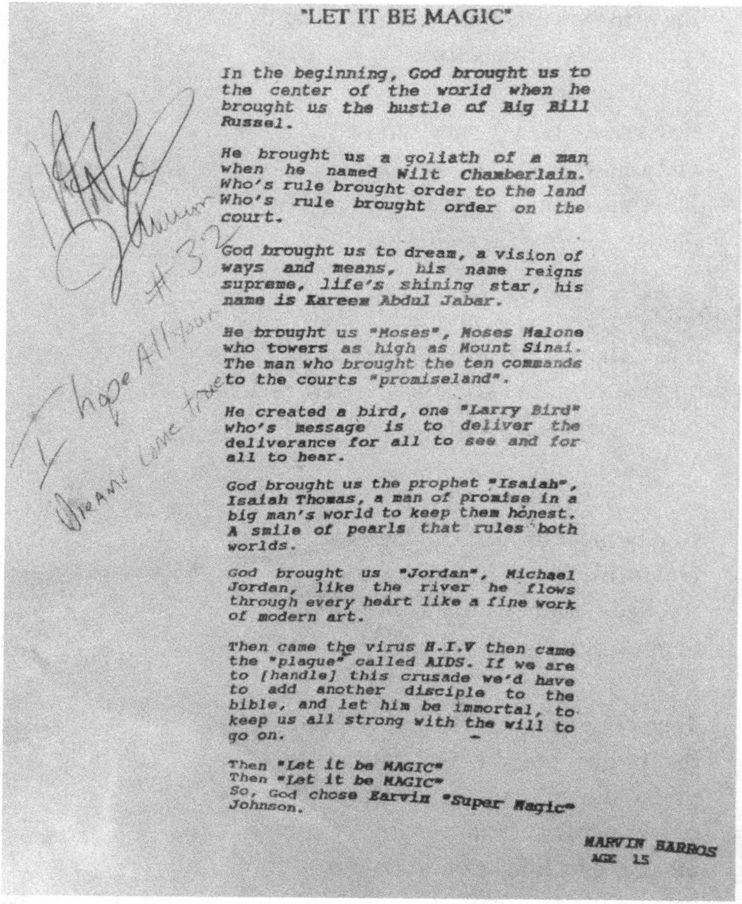

Figure 2.6 "Let It Be Magic," by Marvin Barros Jr.
Source: Courtesy of Doris Barros.

Eric Paulding, the other young man whose face adorns the Community Awareness Tournament banner, was only a high school student in 1997 when, in one of Boston's most violent neighborhoods, he was murdered with one gunshot to the chest. According to news reports, he was an aspiring teacher who participated in Harvard University's Franklin Summer Program where he mentored marginalized youth. One Harvard student who knew Eric well explained, "What most Harvard students probably don't realize is that Eric has been involved with Harvard probably longer than any one of us students."[9] Yet Eric could not escape the violent reach of the gangs. Apparently out of their jealousy, gang members shot him at point-blank range as he left his beloved girlfriend's house.

Eric was Russell's cousin, and for the Community Awareness Tournament, Russell created a video to express his intent. The film opens with a frame of ascending clouds, as if the viewer is being pulled violently toward the heavens. Clouds then cover a sky awash in rain as the sorrowful words of soulful R & B singer Jim Jones bellow through the background: "Nigga, we too close, can't stop praying now. Though it seems there's no end to this pain. Every time I close my eyes I pray for rain. I pray for rain to wash away the strain . . . You couldn't understand how much the pain weigh. So in the hood we love the rainy days, 'cause subconsciously we know the sun's coming."[10] As the song continues to call for the healing waters of rain, the words "In the memory of Marvin Barros and Eric Paulding" flash across the clouds. Then the pictures of others who have died far too young in the streets—James Lee Teal and Tyrus Elijah Sanders—appear on the screen with the words "rest in peace." Russell begins to speak about the purpose of his tournament: "I'm representing my brother and my cousin . . . Community Awareness is to let people know about what's going on in our world, from AIDS and HIV all the way down to heart failure, all the way up to just people in everyday life not knowing to get a check-up, not knowing what's going on with their body . . . that's why we call it Community

Awareness. Everybody enjoys themselves, no fights, no violence . . .
no detail [police], only one cop, almost a thousand people. That
speaks volumes. It's our fifth year, we haven't had any issues." Then
the video cuts to actual footage of games with the icon "Highlight
Heaven" on the bottom-right corner of the screen, the name of the
local video-production company that helped produce the short
film. Intermittently, between the highlights of street ballers catching alley-oop dunks and performing blazing crossover moves, the
video cuts to people reminiscing about Marvin Barros Jr.'s life and
how he helped them.

Then the most solemn moment of the film: Russell kneels down
at the gravesites of Marvin Barros Jr. and Eric Paulding as the song
"I'm Missing You," by Diana Ross, plays in the background. A black
hood over his head, he touches each headstone and blows a kiss
goodbye. There is silence. In the next segment, Russell laments the
disproportionate premature deaths of black boys in the streets and
questions God's benevolence: "People are not dying like they're supposed to. I know God has a will . . . but give life a chance." As the
film ends we see Russell gesture toward the basketball court: "All
our problems and answers are right here. We can solve all our own
issues. We need to work together doing it. And if I can be a big part
of that and I can help in any way possible, that's what I'm going to
do until the day that I go upstairs, man, that's what I'm going to do."
The film fades to Sam Cooke's "A Change Is Gonna Come": "It's
been too hard living but I'm afraid to die. Cause I don't know what's
up there beyond the sky. It's been a long, a long time coming, but I
know a change gonna come, oh yes it will."[11]

During Russell's tournament players express a range of emotions.
At halftime, he calls forth the mothers and family members of Marvin Barros Jr. and Eric Paulding in order to acknowledge their loss
and to show them that their loved ones have not been forgotten:
"Everyone has to come into the gym," explained Russell. "The intention is y'all are the reason why we're here. I want to let you guys

Figure 2.7   Community Awareness Tournament Banner.
Source: Courtesy of Russell Paulding.

know that we haven't forgot as a community. I haven't forgotten as a brother, a cousin, a friend, and this is for y'all. Every year I try to give that up. So the community comes in the gym, claps, you hear some cries, you hear some 'I can't believe it's been ten years, twelve years, fifteen years, a year,' whatever it is, they do that and then people lose their mind and [it's] definitely emotional, but it's something that has to be done because every year so far there's been a different face on that banner. Those are the main two between Eric and Marvin Barros, but I always put an extra friend on there who I've lost throughout the year."

The Community Awareness Basketball Tournament is one of the most emotionally charged and electrifying experiences of the summer. In 2014, I was allowed to play in the tournament, and being in that space, dedicated to my late best friend, helped me release some of the guilt and pain I had carried with me for all those years.

Following the Community Awareness Basketball Tournament comes the Louis Saunders Memorial Tournament, which often takes place at Madison Park High School in Roxbury. The Louis Saunders Memorial Tournament is organized by James Hall and dedicated to his late mentor. Hall also involves Louis Saunders's son, Anthony, who often shares his father's legacy with the crowd to

Figure 2.8 Louis Saunders Tournament Banner.
Source: Photo by author.

open up these games. One local writer describes the opening ritual
for the tournament: "A moment of silence was held, a moment to
Louis Saunders's memory and legacy. At that moment, you might
have heard the sound of basketballs being dribbled; that was actually a thousand heartbeats thumping in memory and in tribute."[12]
The tournament brings together Boston's inner-city community,

Figure 2.9 Louis Saunders Memorial Tournament T-Shirt.
Source: Photo by author.

local street-ball players, teams from other cities in the Northeast, and professional ballplayers for a weekend of intense competition.

The Suave Life Tournament, which comes next, is dedicated to the Mattapan murder victims (see chapter 1). During these games, a banner with the faces of the victims hangs on the steel beams guarding the court. It reads "In Loving Memory."

Two moments during the 2012 Suave Life Basketball Tournament illustrate the ongoing tension between street violence and the search for something greater in Boston street basketball. The sun baked the blacktop as the black-skinned bodies rhythmically turned and twisted with the ball across the court. The tournament was held at Malcolm X Park in front of a raucous crowd. The sunken court at Malcolm X Park is defined by cement walls and raised iron beams. All walks of life from the local community stood hugged against the iron, their faces pressed between the gaps in the fence. There were ballplayers waiting impatiently for their turn to cross the threshold from the intermediate ring and to jump down onto the asphalt stage. Motorcycle riders rested on bikes after being chased by police down side streets or popped wheelies at sixty miles per hour along the main road for the entertainment of the crowd. An older woman sold homemade slushies for a dollar to the children playing on the sidelines, as they dreamed of playing ball at center court. Food trucks blared their sirens and emitted inviting aromas of fried chicken and fries in the hot air. Every so often, the crowd erupted into ear-piercing applause, which from a distance sounded like an ocean of waves crashing against the shore. There were so many people around the first three sides of the court that it was difficult to see the action inside. However, the fourth side of the fence, near the back of the basketball court, remained conspicuously empty.

To the casual observer, the absence of audience members along an entire side of the blacktop made little sense. This was especially true since that side of the park was shaded from the hot sun. But there were obvious reasons for avoiding that side of the asphalt. Just behind the trees were gang members and hustlers, slightly hidden from view. Perched on the rocks and small hills resting in between the trees, these young men were gambling on the games, smoking marijuana, and drinking alcohol. Their presence raised the stakes for the fans and especially for the athletes who were playing for teams that hailed from neighborhoods represented by specific gangs.

As I leaned on the fence next to Baron, it became clear to me that the gang presence was affecting the performances of two ballplayers. Both Marques and Paul were playing for the Stone Hill projects team. Stone Hill was getting crushed by the Mason Street team, and in the process Marques was losing his status as a "known" ballplayer. In order to save his reputation with gang members from Stone Hill projects in the crowd, Marques decided to turn this game into a performance of toughness and masculine prowess. When the ball was put in play, he snatched it out of the air and charged toward the basket hard, head down, muscles flexed, determined to punish whoever got in his way. When he lost the ball and the referee did not call a foul, he glared in his direction and stalked down the court in a rage: "Call the fucking foul!" On the next play, Marques retrieved the ball and raced down the court. He took the ball directly toward his defender, crossed over in one sharp motion from right to left, and made a sweeping jump step to get inside the lane under the basket. He must have been only five-feet-seven-inches tall, but in that moment his body seemed to burst at the seams. As he gathered himself to lift off from the pavement, two sweaty hands gripping the ball, an opposing player hacked down hard, slapping Marques's forearms instead of the basketball. A loud "pap!" reverberated throughout the crowd. The whistle blew, but Marques was already unbuttoned. He stomped around the court, glaring at refs and other players. His clenched his fists and mumbled words under his breadth. His team was down by double digits (they had effectively lost), yet it was clear that Marques had much more to lose than the game. Still irate, he stepped to the free-throw line and managed to will two shots into the basket. One of his teammates called a time-out from the worn wooden benches nailed into the concrete floor on the sidelines.

Instead of joining his teammates, however, Marques stomped angrily toward the crowd. "This is bullshit!" he yelled so fans would notice. Then in a symbolic gesture of his desire to exchange his athletic identity for a "street" identity, he tore off his basketball uniform, displaying a six-pack of stomach muscles and protruding dark chest. Marques sat down in the crowd, signifying his new status. Through the movement of his body on the court and into the crowd, he displaced one masculine role and occupied another. He implicitly understood the "rules of the game," and this was his attempt to salvage a respectable status among peers. Given the limited identity options available to him, it was an ingenious calculation designed to maximize his capital in the neighborhood.

During the time-out, some of Marques's teammates followed suit and tried to distance themselves from the injury to their masculine status this embarrassing loss had produced. While sitting on the bench, Paul lambasted another teammate, yelling loud enough for the crowd to hear: "You play like a girl, fucking pussy. Fuck that!" reclaiming his masculinity in misogynistic terms.

Eventually the referee blew the whistle for players to return to the court. When Marques heard the sound he slowly put his jersey back on and walked onto the asphalt. He was obviously experiencing some level of role ambiguity. As the ball moved up and down the court at a rapid pace, Marques moved slowly, his attention caught between the crowd and the game. When the final whistle blew he immediately walked over to several audience members to complain about the referees and the outcome of the game. As I watched his performance unfold, I turned to Baron. "Baron," I asked, "what do you think was happening there?" Baron turned to me and whispered: "Onaje, the number one killer out here is pride."

The Suave Life Tournament games were informative and a few hours later I decided to jump down onto the asphalt where I could obtain a better view. When I landed on the blacktop, several onlookers were already crowding beneath the basket, their toes almost touching the baseline. One of the main differences between street basketball and more organized games is the loose boundaries between audience members and players. Whereas in more organized settings interactions between observers and players are discouraged, in street basketball they are an essential part of the contest.

During heated games, audience members literally stand around sidelines, sometimes forming a human out-of-bounds-line. Without warning, one of these onlookers might feel compelled to jump onto the court to dance or to make fun of a player in the game.

Players too, go into the audience to celebrate, gloat, or even to cry. These interactions are infectious, and over time the rhythmic call-and-response between players and audience members generates an intensely shared experience. One rare but clear example of this in professional basketball was film director Spike Lee's famous back-and-forth banter with Hall of Fame NBA players such as Michael Jordan and Reggie Miller at Madison Square Garden. Of course, Spike Lee is familiar with the street-basketball subculture, having directed a film on urban basketball in New York City where the main player is a savior named "Jesus Shuttlesworth."[13] Spike Lee is especially well known for talking trash to Reggie Miller during the 1995 NBA Eastern Conference finals, which pushed Miller to score eight points in the final eleven seconds to beat the Knicks. Nevertheless, the difference between an NBA game and street basketball is that fans do not have to be millionaires to have intimate contact with players.

When I dropped down onto the court, I noticed a friend from years earlier, who had been standing on the baseline all along. He talked loudly and held a bottle covered in a brown paper bag. Between comments, he sipped the bottle and busted into loud conversations or screamed at players on the court. I walked toward him. He noticed me immediately and slapped my outstretched hand: "Naje, what's up my nigga? Yo, I heard you writing a book on basketball. I was thinking about this the other day. You know how some nigga from one gang, be playing with a nigga from another gang. And because they playing on the same team, right, they become cool. Like yo, I was coaching two cats from different gangs and I saw them on the bus and before it would have been a fight, but yo, they had respect for each other because of basketball. Yo, Naje, you got to find a way to work that shit into your book, yo for real, man!" I told him I would try to mention it.

Almost as soon he said those words the crowd erupted in frenzy: "Ohhhhhh shit!" A light-skinned, left-handed ball player with a handsome face had gone the length of the right side of the blacktop, jumped off the asphalt, hung in the air, leaned sideways with his right side toward the basket, and dunked on somebody's head. It felt like the air had been sucked out of the place. My friend, who had been facing the court, almost spilled his beer. He screamed in with the entire crowd. People were holding their mouths saying "Oh my God" and the noise reached such a crescendo that, suddenly, I felt like I was in a different world. The young man who performed the dunk was staring right at us as he began running back down the court on defense: "Yo," my friend screamed in his direction, "I see you, my nigga! I see you!" The dunker responded: "I told you, my nigga! I told you!" In that moment of recognition, an individual dunk had become a shared experience. Within the euphoria I felt connected to everyone at the park, including my drunken friend who could not keep his beer from spilling to the ground. I cherished that sense of belonging because, at least for a time, we had left the ghetto behind us.

Once the Suave Life Tournament is over, Boston's street-basketball community moves to the location of the C-Murder Tournament, dedicated to the memory of a young man nicknamed C-Murder who was killed while trying to break up a fight between two men in the streets. "That was my boy. He didn't bother no one," explained the organizer of the tournament. "He was actually just trying to calm things down and ended up getting killed. He was a good man!"

Subsequent to the C-Murder Tournament is the Melvia Wright Patten Tournament, which used to be held in the infamous Bromley-Heath Street projects, home to one of the city's most violent gangs. Melvia Wright Patten was the director of the Bromley-Heath Infant and Toddler Daycare Center and became well known as the "mother" and caregiver of Bromley-Heath's children. She was an educated woman, deeply committed to changing the lives of marginalized youth through her love and dedication to teaching. Once she passed away, her son Marvin, who is now a Boston Police officer, created the tournament to celebrate her legacy of teaching Boston's inner-city youth. Through sponsorship and community support, the tournament helps generate $5,000 each year for Boston city youth to attend institutions of higher learning. The tournament was recently moved to the Franklin Field housing projects, home to another notorious Boston gang.

In May 2010, a fourteen-year-old honors student, Jaewon Martin (not affiliated with the Melvia Wright Patten Tournament), was shot to death on the Bromley-Heath Street project's basketball court. According to news reports, two rival gang members mistook Martin for a Heath Street gang member. As Martin and his friends played ball, the killers approached and shot him in the chest. When his friends ran, gang members followed and shot at them as well, wounding one.

The *Boston Globe* reported that after Martin's murder, community members turned the basketball court into a makeshift memorial shrine. Streams of residents stopped by half-court to place teddy bears, candles, and other special items. At the time, the Bromley-Heath community center director suggested that the basketball court was a place where Martin's friends "can go back and probably talk to Jaewon." One young man named Anthony Upchurch grabbed a basketball and shot jump shots in honor of Martin: "It was his way of honoring the 14-year-old eighth grader, who played on the same court."[14] It is difficult to say why the community chose center court to build a shrine for Martin. Of course, in many religious traditions, the center point between the four cardinal directions symbolizes the meeting place between the sacred and the profane. Although the Melvia Wright Patten Tournament technically ends Boston's calendar of street-ball tournaments, new tournaments always arise. In the summer of 2013, for example, there was the Merrill Court "Fathers Are Champions Too" Basketball Tournament. The organizers designed the tournament with fathers and sons playing back-to-back games.

Figure 2.10 Jaewon Martin Memorial, Roxbury, May 2010.
Source: Photograph by Yoon S. Byun, "Playing Scared: A Neighborhood Reflects as Teen Killed on Court Is Mourned," *Boston Globe*, May 12, 2010. Courtesy of the *Boston Globe*.

I made the pilgrimage through Boston's memorial games each summer and learned that these contests expressed far more than a search for the American dream. After all, these tournaments were not named after NBA stars. They were dedicated to African Americans, most of them men and most of them young, killed violently and before their time. In this sense, Boston street basketball had become a way of life, a set of practices arising out of these young men's lived experiences. The participants were wrestling with existential questions on the court: What is the meaning of death? What happens to murder victims after they die? Are these people still with us, and if so, how should they be acknowledged? What does it mean to be a mother, father, daughter, or son in the absence

Figure 2.11 Merrill Court Tournament T-Shirt.
Source: Photo by author.

of intact families? What is God's plan and do I have a purpose? These young men had performed their collective histories on the court, turning their bodies into altars of the past in the hope of a future without violence.

PART 2

HOPE

3

JASON, HOOPS, AND GRANDMA'S HANDS

For Jason, basketball is hope. Whenever he touches the ball, something like the will to live is pulled out of him and put on sparkling display. In the first half of one of our games, Jason dove to the hoop, yelling, "Ah, feed me!" When he didn't get the ball, he continued running under the basket, circling back to the top of the key, hands outstretched, calling for the rock. I delivered the ball with a crisp chest pass from the left wing, following through with my fingers to make sure it reached his shooting pocket. Jason stepped into the pass and snatched the ball in midair, then pivoted toward the hoop to face his opponent. Staring into his defender's eyes, Jason dribbled two steps backward, drawing his opponent farther from the hoop. I could tell that he wanted to dance with this man. With the crowd enthralled and Jason and his defender locked in battle, he initiated a flurry of crossover dribbles at his opponent's feet. The tall and muscular player guarding Jason moved his body to the beat of the ball, keeping his head up and arms outstretched, his legs in constant motion. As I stood on the wing, it seemed that neither player would break the intimacy of their rhythmic intertwine. Then, in the flow of Jason's final crossover, he hesitated between the beat, throwing his defender off rhythm. Jason swung the ball to his right hand and glided past, leaving the baller in his wake. Jason bolted toward the rim and finished with his left hand over a six-foot-eleven center that had jumped straight up in the air with both hands to block Jason's shot. Given the hundreds of people in the crowd that day, it was a courageous play by a ballplayer with an indomitable spirit.

Jason is six-foot-four and muscular, twenty-four years old with dark smooth skin and a gleaming bald head. I first noticed him during a pick-up game in one of Boston's city gyms. He seemed like a crazed man with a basketball, racing around the court. Every time he came down from the sky with a defensive rebound, he bolted down the hardwood, whiplashing his opponents on the way. "Ah, ah!" he yelled when he crossed one of them over. I noticed he had two favorite spots for pull-up jump shots with his right hand: the top of the key and the short corner along the right baseline. The rhythm of his game was frenetic. It sounded like "bop, bop, bop, bopbopbopbop, uh, snap" through the net. In all the games I have watched Jason play since then, very few guys could keep up with him on the court.

The way Jason moved his body intrigued me. I wondered what story was behind his game. While I was completing my graduate studies and Jason was struggling to survive in Boston, we became brothers; so much time on the basketball court together created a bond between us. That bond gave Jason the courage to share his story of hope through hoops.

PICKED ME UP

Grandma's hands
Picked me up each time I fell
Grandma's hands
Boy, they really came in handy . . .

But I don't have Grandma anymore

If I get to Heaven I'll look for
Grandma's hands
　　—Bill Withers, "Grandma's Hands"

To understand Jason's hope through hoops is to appreciate the basketball court as a meeting place infused with his great-grandmother's spirit. Jason's mother has been a crack addict since he was born. His father is unavailable. His aunts and uncles are drug addicts and hustlers. His entire family, in fact, is a legacy of poverty, urban decay, and the war on drugs. Recognizing terror in Jason's future, his great-grandmother cuddled him in her arms when he was a baby before she died. She was a deeply religious woman with a devoted prayer life. She sang to him often:

Are we weak and heavy-laden,
Cumbered with a load of care?
Precious Savior, still our refuge—
Take it to the Lord in prayer.
Do thy friends despise, forsake thee?
Take it to the Lord in prayer!
In His arms He'll take and shield thee,
Thou wilt find a solace there.[1]

When she died, Jason had to move in with his crack-addicted mother, but he never forgot his great-grandmother's song: the Lord would deliver him in His arms and give him solace there. I asked Jason to tell me what his great-grandmother's words meant to him. She "put something into me" that was "not of this world," he explained.

She—mind you my great-grandmother, like to this day I think about her. I want to just drop a tear because how that connection that I have with her for those years at the beginning of my life. Those few years of my life it was just so—it's crazy like you know she always—like I was just meant to be in her arms and she was meant to just give me something. I got

something from her. I just don't know what it is. Whatever I
got from my great-grandmother is the reason why I'm on the
road where I'm at now. For some reason at my age right now
I'm completely aware that you can't live for the things of the
world, and it's just so crazy 'cause the things that God has put
in my life and that I've been through for these twenty-four
years of my life, it's like he's getting me ready for something.
You know what I mean, and whatever it was that I got from
my great-grandmother I still feel it now when I think about it.

That feeling of ultimate purpose never left Jason, despite the anger
of not having a father in his life or of constantly moving between
government housing projects and foster homes. When Jason and I
first met, he was homeless, unable to live in the apartment where
his mother smoked drugs. While I taught an adjunct course in eth-
ics at Roxbury Community College to support my graduate work,
Jason and I worked it out so that he could make a few dollars and
stay warm by watching my son in my heated car. One cold winter
morning he barely made it to the car after spending the whole night
outside. My wife and I struggled for several weeks to find him an
apartment and a job. Even then, basketball and hope kept him from
giving up. "I know I'm going through this for a reason," he told me,
"so that one day I can use basketball to tell my story and to lift the
spirits of people who are suffering."

When they were adolescents, Jason told his cousin that he had
just seen his cousin's mother buy crack cocaine. Shame and denial
washed over his cousin's face and the revelation caused an unspo-
ken pain between the two boys. As Jason explained to me, however, it was more than just pain. It felt evil, as if a spiritual force
had insinuated itself within his family, holding them hostage to
the demons of the inner city. During our conversations before and
after games, Jason would tell me, "Onaje, it's not my mother who is
treating me so bad. I know something has a hold on her. I know it!"

Eventually, Jason internalized those demons in terms of his own anger, frustration, and depression. As he explained, there were demons in the family.

> Me and my cousins we grew up watching how can I say the generation above us dealing with a lot of demons individually, mostly all the same and at a young age we would find ourselves subdued to a certain perspective of life. Me and my cousins being of the same age, around the same age some of them find themselves—you know just because you're around—when you're around something a lot you become that and they found themselves joining in terms of getting angry fast and not knowing what to do. Confusion, depression at a young age, that's where it all starts in adolescence. For instance with my cousin, the one that I told you that was stabbed eleven times, he introduced me to basketball and a lot of his pain was my pain because he was more of a role model to me. To see him go through that it's like just a certain feeling of how I seen how real life was right there and I remember telling him that—he didn't want to believe it. I remember at first telling him that my aunt, his mother, that yo man, somebody just sold her drugs. He looked at me like what? 'Get out of here' . . . The feeling of dealing with my personal issues with, you know how my mother treated me because of drugs because my mother also do drugs too still to this day and battling her demons . . . Them growing up in Boston at a young age they had me at a young age. Losing family members they all have demons that hopped on their back at a young age you know 'cause back in the eighties, the eighties was tough.

In the midst of his dread, Jason sought out a spiritual refuge on the basketball court. For some reason, the asphalt gave him access to the original feelings of innocence and purpose he first felt in his great-grandmother's arms. The basketball court served as a maternal substitute, an enduring presence of God's love: "On that court I was by myself and unconsciously I would leave my house with my mother yelling at me. My counselor was that and I would talk to that, to the hoop, to the ball, to the sky. . . . That was God's way of showing me his love."

Jason explained that on the basketball court he felt safe enough to express his pain. Sometimes his eyes were so red from crying on the court that when he returned home from playing ball his family thought he had smoked marijuana. He poured his heart out on the asphalt.

> I love my family as a whole. In a way their life I felt was mine, and that pain that they gave me by the hating . . . it got to the point where I needed . . . Subliminally basketball ended up becoming something that I projected all my stress from 'cause it was the only thing that just cleared my mind from everything that was going on in the world, when I'm on that court, and it all started at a young age. . . . It took me a while to realize it obviously 'cause the devil put enemies in strange places, and I love my mother to death but he was working on my mom since the beginning. That was what honestly really got me started into just going to the court unconsciously. I would go to the court and eat ["eat" is a slang word that means, in this case, to feed on life or the vital source of life]. I'm telling you dawg. I will go to the court and I eat, come back, my eyes are red. You think that I'm like—I'm just getting high off of basketball. I come home and she's like yeah, you smoking weed 'cause you leaving the crib already cause she's making you mad and you come back, but yeah like it—and the thing is I did that unconsciously.

Jason survived his early childhood years and the family curse, in part, by releasing his pain through basketball. Hoops became the center of his personality and gave him a sense of purpose. It also offered him something like a divine calling—a special alternative to the usual pathways to prison and death that his friends were on.

> I didn't really realize that that was my gift, one of my gifts that's given from God at that age and from that point on, from middle school and that whole high school whatever my objective was to be something more. I have something to do. I'm in school enjoying it. People appreciate me as a person all around than just African American, typically oppressed. So you know I'm looking back at that and just that whole transition from being the suckiest player to then becoming that guy, but those people that was trying to belittle me and be condescending was the butt suckers at the end of it all. When I look at it it's just like I've seen within myself what basketball meant. Basketball showed me how when you believe in something, basketball literally just mapped it out in terms of how can I say it, like when you believe in something in terms of proving yourself that you can reach a certain level, that's what basketball did at a young age.

By the time Jason was a high school senior, he was the star player on his team and one of the most popular students at school. His troubles at home were masked by the glow of the hoops' spotlight. Although his college applications were initially denied, eventually a local Division III college scout approached him. He explained how much he appreciated Jason's talents and invited him to consider enrolling in his school. Jason became the first person in his family to attend college, partly as a result of that meeting: "I remember just being like, I'm going to college. You know what I'm saying? Nobody in my family—I didn't even know what that was. There was nothing above me to show me what it was. I'm like, I'm going to college."

COLLEGE TRANSFORMATION

Jason's freshman year in college was the first time he began to realize that forces other than God and personal suffering had played a role in his dream to play basketball. He also became aware of serving the interests of a predominately white college and student body who were simultaneously fascinated and suspicious of his black male body. Women assumed his sexual prowess and treated him like a piece of meat. His white coach viewed him as a prized property, valuable but only insofar as he was able to produce winning results on the basketball court. To the larger university culture, Jason was the stereotype of typically gifted black athlete.

Jason loved the attention and maybe even enjoyed performing the myth of his new status as a freshman: "My freshman year I was basically trying to live out what I thought it was about at first and that was going to school, having fun 'cause it was fun from the jump. Going to school, having fun playing basketball, the girls, partying. It was like yeah, we was runnin' things. Like yo we be nice!" But the cultural fantasy shaping Jason's identity came crashing down before the season even began. An observant physical trainer noticed Jason stretching awkwardly on the sidelines. She pulled him aside after practice and suggested an MRI after stiffness in his hips. Jason was torn apart by the results. His hips were severely arthritic, required surgery, and he might not ever play basketball again. Tears rolled down his face:

> She sat me down just like a movie, dawg, just like a movie right then and there. Something that I love passionately, that I thought I loved passionately, that I thought I was embracing and it was taken away just like that. She said you can't, you're not cleared to play because you have a rare form of arthritis called—I don't even remember the name of this. Threw it out

as soon as I found out I was healed by God I threw it out, but she said you have a rare form of arthritis and your hip joint is fused. If you do not have surgery before the age of twenty-five she said you're going to have to have a hip replacement, that's what she said. I sat there and my jaw dropped and I just started crying like a little punk, just like a baby. Just like a baby I started crying. It hit me hard.

Jason wasn't aware of it at first, but his illness signaled the beginning of a transformation in his self-perception from a stereotypical black athlete to a ballplayer with a more liberated consciousness. In fact, Jason's surgery stirred up dangerous memories of his past, of that original feeling of ultimate worth he first shared with his great-grandmother.

After the first surgery failed to correct his arthritic condition, Jason's doctor scheduled a second attempt, fortuitously, on Jason's great-grandmother's birthday. Upon waking up in the recovery room after the successful surgery, Jason peered over toward the corner of the room. He noticed two spirits standing there watching him in the shadows against the wall. One, he was sure, was his great-grandmother. She had orchestrated the whole ordeal to awaken him from his cultural slumber. All he could feel and say in that moment as he stared at her apparition was "Thank you, thank you!"

I'm in this room then mom was just sitting there talking and I'm telling you dawg I like want to drop a tear thinking about it. I'm in the room, I'm just saying thank you. I want to fly. I don't know why I'm saying thank you. Why? Just thank you and I started crying. I just said thank you and I started crying. I remember looking over to the right side of the room. I put this on and I put this on every day that ignites my existence. I see two shadows over there, a tall one and a short one. I didn't know what the tall one was but I know that short one was my

great-grandmother, and I was just saying damn and I was saying thank you. I was just crying, saying thank you. I don't even
know why. I don't have not a clue why.

This ecstatic moment represented another awakening for Jason, a
turning point away from the symbolic cage of race and masculinity toward something "more," something ineffable: "I took a deep
breath and from that I'm like a different—I'm psyched. I don't
know what was put in me after that. Something is just different. It's
like I had a whole different feeling to life. I was aware of something.
I didn't know what it was. It's kind of a different awareness."

While in the hospital bed, Jason found the courage to tell his
mother about his dream of leaving the ghetto and playing professional basketball. He told her that God had come to him "in broken
spirits" in the hospital and given him a new way to use basketball for
others. For months, Jason thought about how his relationship with
basketball might change. For one, he was committed, as he put it,
to "give no man dominion over me," especially his college basketball coach, whom he had given too much authority. He was now
intent on exercising his own spiritual agency on the court despite
the indignities he had suffered from his coach and the culture of the
university. Jason also decided that he would no longer rely on racial
fantasies of his natural athletic talent to accrue status, have sexual
conquests, or gain the paternalistic favor of white coaches. He had
moved from a false sense of masculinity to a more authentic sense of
manhood. Jason was developing his own version of a hoops' theology of liberation.

That God—think about it, that God gave me this talent. He
gave me this gift. He gave me the opportunity to be in school,
not my coach, not my teachers, not any human being that
walks the earth with me, therefore they have no power over
me. You get what I'm saying? When I became fully alert of

that nothing was stopping me on the campus. I was the man because I am blessed in His name. Before I was the man in a different way but I knew I was the man in a humble, modest, sincere kind way. You feel what I'm saying?

As Jason became more alert to the power dynamics involved in hoops, he realized his own agency. He became determined to surrender freedom to no one but God, both on or off the court:

Something that God has given me, [the coach] he's telling me not to do this and I'm looking at it like hold on, hold on. I looked up to you as a father, as a father figure. You gave me an opportunity but that was my mistake. Allow no man to have dominion over you. That's written. That was my mistake. He took that and he abused it because of his bitterness as a person.

Over the next three basketball seasons, Jason struggled to resolve his desire to play ball and his need to defy his coaches' limitations. This struggle between his old, narrowly defined consciousness, represented by the authority of his coach and the university, and his new, more expansive consciousness, catalyzed by his encounter with his great-grandmother's spirit in the hospital bed, was so intense that he chose not to play basketball for the college team during the next three years. His coach may have allowed him to return to the team sooner, but Jason could not bring himself to play for a man that devalued him as a human being. Moreover, Jason needed to take time away from his coach in order to relearn his own worth. He found a job and focused on his education. Then one day he met a special woman, a "lady of God" who would eventually help him return to the basketball court.

That summer I met this lady that was a friend of my mother's and she's a lady of God, a voice of God you could say, and she thought that she was coming to my house for my mother and it's like to bless the house. We've come to the recollection that she was brought for me and around that time I met her. She told me "you want to play basketball again?" She said "you going to play basketball again." She said "you also going to find a job." This woman when she told me that I was like, "for the league?" She was like, "nah, you want to play basketball again?" She said "I don't see professional," and for some reason all I needed to hear was her say you're going to get back on the court even though she didn't say professional. I said I'm going professional. I just did it and for some reason like the way she said it to me 'cause when she came and said all she could do was stare. She was staring at me. I didn't know. I didn't know why. I didn't know what was going on, but this woman she was sent into my life to tell me that message.

Jason later discovered that Dora was of Afro-Caribbean descent and that she could hear messages from two "African West Indian spirits." Ancestor spirits, this time through Dora, had once again intervened with concern for Jason's relationship to hoops.

When the summer was over, Jason went to his coach's office to discuss the upcoming season. He was now a senior, and it would be his final opportunity to play college ball. To his surprise, his coach accepted Jason back on the team, albeit in a reduced role on the bench. But his lowly place on the depth chart didn't bother Jason as much. This time he wasn't playing for his coach but for himself. During the season, Jason played an important role in his team's success. They finished the year with a winning record. There were no signs of the arthritic condition that had kept Jason on the sidelines three years before. He had been "healed by God," he explained, evidenced by his ability to play above the rim. But, for him, the culmination of his three years of soul-searching occurred in one of the final games of the season.

EVERYTHING CAME OUT IN THE GAME

The night before the game, Jason's cousin almost died on Roxbury's streets, stabbed eleven times. A few days before, Jason and his cousin had a huge argument and that was the last time Jason had seen him. Now his cousin could be dead. Jason could hardly sleep that evening after he visited his cousin in the hospital, tears in his eyes. In the morning, he went to class, but up until game time thoughts of his cousin's near-murder swirled through his mind. "Why? Why are we dying? Why can't we escape the pain? Why God?" Jason put on his uniform and bent down to tie up his white laces. After taking a deep breath, he tried to gather himself and walked out of the tunnel onto the court surrounded by screaming fans. When the first warm-up ball bounced toward his hands, several thoughts went through his mind: his great-grandmother, her everlasting song, mother's drug addiction, absent father, foster homes, surgery, abusive coach, wounded cousin, all of it.

From the beginning of the game going to shoot around after stretching, listening to music, getting suited and booted I remember going down early and stretching and I remember just having first of all already being mad about how he tried to bench me the first time. All I remember is when I was shooting around it was just like still saying what the heck is going on because I was traumatized by that little bit in terms of how real it is. When this emotion, the type of emotion you have for a loved one despite how you all argue or—because I remember before the last time I spoke to my cousin it was an argument. So he could have died and we would have ended it like that. That was going through my mind while we was throwing around. I just remember this being like—and then as it started coming—like when I started getting into that feeling it started coming back to when we first started playing basketball as a family and how we just talked about Paul Pierce and just going on because I always wanted to be better than him. And he would be yeah, it's getting real, me and him and his brother and that type of energy from that part of my life with basketball. It was like that love that I have for that part of my life and the love I had for him and then as a whole the pain that we had to deal with as a family. That was the cherry on top and then everything that came to my head about why I was playing basketball came out in the game.

At the start of the game, when the ball left the referee's hand, all of Jason's pain came out on the court. Telling his story in public with his body was cathartic. Suddenly his mind went to another place beyond the crowd:

> I got tired a little bit but I told you all I had to do was just breathe. I'm just going to keep playing. This warm feeling just came over me. Like I don't care. I'm telling you, I didn't pay attention to who was in the crowd. I didn't even pay attention to the coach. It was just I was on that floor. I remember just being on that floor and it was just basketball. There was nothing outside of that. I heard but I didn't even know who it was. I looked over to the bench one time. I was just numb to the surroundings. I was playing, it was a beautiful thing. I was just playing.

Jason jerked his body as he sat in the chair across from me and told me his story. He was back there in the gym, playing. He flicked his wrist, shot the ball and said: "that's for the pain!" Then a dribbling motion. "That's for my cousin." Then a behind the back, cross-over. "That's for the drugs." He was narrating his story through hoops.

As the final buzzer drew near, Jason felt an enormous need to thank God for the depth of meaning that he was able to encounter on the court. He exclaimed to me: "there will never, ever be someone like me to touch that court!"

After everything—first of all getting a win 'cause we needed a win. Everything man, God was just showing me. He was just showing me that I will give it to you. I prayed for it. I was crying to Him like a baby crying for his mother. He kept my cousin here. It's my senior year at college. I mentioned my senior year at college I'm going to start on the basketball team, double, doubles or whatever you want to call it but I just came off the bench. I scored seventeen points and those seventeen points, we won by what, thirteen? So I'm just like—but then looking at that then all that pain, it was like all that pain, that's everything. I just thought about every emotional hit that I had to deal with my family and peers and life. Right there it was like just saying thank you for letting me stand where I'm standing right now. Thank you for just listening to me. Thank you for getting me through all that pain, all that confusion. Just thank you for all that.

I started crying dawg 'cause looking at that court, looking at everything I've been through on that basketball court I put this on everything. There would never, ever be somebody like me to touch that court. I'm just, look I'm standing on this court and it's like, yo, dawg this is crazy. It's so crazy like I'm standing right here still doing it. Like I'm doing it right now. I started crying dawg.

The trainer who had diagnosed Jason's arthritic condition happened to be present at this game. As tears rolled down Jason's face, he looked over at the bench and noticed her crying. Her recognition filled Jason with joy. Once again, it was a woman, in a male-dominated sport, who affirmed Jason's true worth as a human being.

> I started crying and when that trainer started, when I seen her crying that was honestly one of the best feelings in my life. Somebody—so she was paying attention to somebody else. She truly, deeply understood because she was there with me when I had to come back, and she started crying the same way I started crying.

Jason's hoop's ritual generated a sense of hope and his story is a testament to the "lived" religious meanings injured black males may experience during the flow of games. Jason began sobbing as we spoke. In his words, and in the solemn silent space between them, I was transported onto the court with him as he felt past sorrows.

Jason's story underscores several points regarding urban basketball as a "lived religion." First, while street basketball may often be concerned with the experiences of black men, it must be connected to the source from which they come—the mothers, grandmothers, and ultimately, the feminine creative energy that is the origin of all life. For Jason, the court is a maternal symbol, a place where he seeks refuge from a hostile world. His story of rebirth through hoops suggests that black male athletes cannot achieve spiritual freedom from the hegemonic forces of culture without realizing the ultimate value of women. Second, his journey through basketball, like those of the vast majority of black men I interviewed, is infused with the presence of ancestor spirits. His is not simply a Christian experience of hoops. Rather, he plays ball at the behest of his great-grandmother's soul and Afro-West Indian spirits. God may be at the apex of Jason's hoops theology, but ancestors mediate God's grace on the court. His religious sensibilities combine Christian and Afro-Caribbean or African sources in which the dead have a continued role among the living and spirit is earthbound and experiential. Finally, I will never forget the moment Jason cried in front of me as he told his story. His vulnerability and trust sealed our relationship. Basketball provided the space for two urban black men to love each other in a way that defied cultural expectations of manliness. Our bond has been a continued source of hope between us ever since.

4

C.J., HOOPS, AND THE QUEST FOR A SECOND LIFE

It still seems to me that my late best friend, Marvin Barros Jr., was the one who led me to reconnect with C.J. "Marvin, I miss you and now that I have found you, I will never let you go!" I cried as I embraced his lifeless body, lost and forgotten in a pile of dirt and leaves in the woods. As I held him, I remembered how he was counselor and friend to both C.J. and me when we were young and growing up in the streets of Roxbury and how my mother had looked at him strangely the first time I brought him to our apartment to stay the night. How at night, due to his hemophilia, Marvin's gums would bleed onto his pillow. Sometimes he'd wake up terrified at the sight of his own blood.

Despite the risks, Marvin would sneak onto the court to play basketball once in a while because he loved the game. When he did, we played half-court, on the same team. He would set up his long and skinny six-foot-four inch frame in the middle of the paint while I stood at the top of the key with the ball. I'd lob a pass over my defender to Marvin and sprint to the right or left of the basket. Then he would step toward me and roll the ball off his fingers so I could scoop it in for a sweet layup. Once in a while, Marvin would fake the pass, turn in the opposite direction and shoot a fadeaway jump shot with his left hand. He moved his body slowly and deliberately, like a praying mantis in sneakers. His joints were swollen and painful. An elbow or kick to his frame often meant a week's stay at the hospital. I would visit, and he and I would race up and down the hallways in stray wheelchairs, eat salty french fries, and play video games all night.

I was devastated when Marvin died the same year I left to play basketball at a prestigious private high school in New Jersey. He called me several nights before his death. "Naj," his voice crackling and sickly over the phone, "you were the reason I did everything. I did it for the kids. I love the kids, and I just wanted to make life better for them." Then he spoke to me softly, "I love you." It was the first time he had said those words to me. He was now twenty-one. I was seventeen. "I love you too," I responded. That was the last time I ever spoke to Marvin before that encounter in the woods, many years later.

"Little Marvin wanted you to have this." Marvin's mother cried as she handed me the gold and silver basketball hoop pendant Marvin used to wear around his neck. When I opened my palm I saw an intricately woven hoop of gold set inside a silver frame, with a silver basketball hovering above the rim. I smiled and clutched the object in my hand. I remembered Marvin's words: "Naj, now I see what you are doing. At first, I didn't understand. I wanted you to dominate and prove that you were the best ballplayer in Roxbury. But now I see what you are doing. You are playing ball for a different reason, to become a better person. Now I understand, man. Keep going!" He had been watching the slow and graceful way that I approached the game, as though it was a moving meditation and I was unconcerned about the world around me. And now he had given me a golden threaded hoop and ball, through his mother. I wondered if it was a sign, the threaded net of the basket signaling the way our lives had been woven together through hoops. Was Marvin speaking beyond the grave? "Keep going through hoops! I will be there with you. Nothing can break the bond between us! Nothing. Not even death!" I hoped so.

So fifteen years after his death, when I discovered Marvin's body, cold and wet, lying in the thick of the woods, I was saddened but not that surprised. I cried and held him close. I apologized for leaving him alone and forgotten as I toiled through college and graduate school. I carried him near a fire burning among a pile of stones and attempted to rekindle his spirit. Then I sat him under an oak tree and fed him water and beer. I sang to Marvin, danced for him, and told him that I wanted to escort him to his resting place. Then as the sun pulled back the darkness of the night, I recognized the first signs of life, ushering him into his new being. I carried his body down to the river and bathed him in morning waters. He lay awake and at peace with me, happy. As Marvin rested, I shared my failings and dreams with him. How to keep going, how to make sense of the ache for meaning black men experienced on basketball courts? Could the game become a tool of liberated consciousness? I asked Marvin to assist me on the journey. "If there is a way," I said, "show me."

I left the woods with hope in my heart, even though I had to return to Boston where some of my graduate school professors didn't think writing a book about religion and basketball was worthwhile. "You have to write white," one professor explained. "I feel protective of you. You are a black man. The academy will stereotype you as just another black man who loves basketball. You need to demonstrate your grasp of theory rather than focusing on a parochial practice like hoops." I was hurt and discouraged. How could I explain to him that I didn't have the privilege of being a disembodied professor? Whatever ideas I professed had to make sense to those who lived in the streets and in black skin. A few days later, another religious studies professor refused to meet with me. "You should really get to know Onaje as a student. He is a really nice young man," a colleague of his suggested. "I don't care. I don't want to know him," he replied. I felt isolated. Although I was earning a Ph.D. at Martin Luther King Jr.'s alma mater, I was the only black male doctoral student in a department lacking professors of color.[1]

Nevertheless, I had traveled too far from the streets of Roxbury to the academy to succumb now. After the woods, I took a subway train to Marvin's old apartment in Roxbury's Mission Hill projects. I wanted to see his mother and younger twin sisters, to be reunited with them. Little Marvin's father—Big Marvin—had died of cancer while grieving for his son.

As I walked up the stairs to their front door my heart was pounding. I knocked; the door opened. His beautiful sister emerged, her face beaming with light. "Onaje, oh my God, is that you? Where have you been? We've been looking all over for you! Come in. Come in. We're not going to lose you again." We spoke for hours, mostly about how life had changed and yet remained the same. As our conversation came to an end, we stood up and embraced. Their mother was not home, but I still felt a weight of guilt and grief lift from my shoulders. I stepped out of their front door into the night, and a cool whistling breeze met my face.

REUNITING WITH C.J.

It was dark; dry leaves swirled through the air. I sauntered down the stairs and onto the main road under dim streetlights. Marvin's house was inside gang territory, but I was unafraid. "Naaaaaje!" a grumbling baritone voice bellowed from nowhere. I looked around. "Naaaaaje!" I could not figure out where the voice was coming from. Then I peered over and down at a small, beat up old black car with holes on the side, which had stopped inconspicuously near a curb on the road. "Yoooo, what's up my nigga! It's C.J.," the voice rumbled. "C.J.! What? C.J.! How have you been?" I asked. "You know, tryin' to maintain, that's all. Just did a bid in prison. Tryin' to get my life back together, you know what I'm sayin'? The struggle life. Matter of fact, I was just talking about you to G-Big, like, 'yo, remember when Naje use to give 'em the business on the bball court?' Definitely though, I want to catch up with you my bro." "Yo C.J.," I responded excitedly. "I just came from Marv's old house! Yo, we're family bro. We grew up together. You lived right down the street from me. Of course, anything I can do man, to be there for you, I'm there. What's your number so I can give you a call and we can meet up?" C.J. rattled off his number and then vanished into the night. I stopped, turned, and gazed at Marvin's old place. "If there is a way, show me," I had once said. Now I wondered if it had begun.

C.J. had been psychologically scarred by death. Through basketball, he was seeking a second life. As children growing up in Roxbury, we were friends. He lived on Maybury Street, down the block from my grandmother's apartment. I remember seeing C.J. rush home from school to retrieve his gym shorts so he could make it to the basketball court on time. On the court, C.J. was quicker and faster than everyone else. Shorter too, which is why he was known as "little C.J." in the neighborhood. Since our apartments were nestled between two gang territories—the Maybury boys and Intervale crew—we walked on the main roads to the Yawkey Club.

C.J. dealt with a crack-addicted and alcoholic father at home. His father was a source of fear and instability for his mother and little sister as well. When C.J. turned seven, his father was imprisoned and he never saw him again. C.J. didn't know which was worse—a drugged-up father at home or losing him to prison: "I had a father up until those ages, until about seven years old. That's why I started ended up going to the boys and girls club. At that age he went to jail. Liquor was in his life. Drugs was in his life. He left the house." The loss of his father to prison pushed C.J. to search for male role models on the local basketball courts. C.J. was short, but he was also ambidextrous. He could bounce the ball with either hand as if it were tied to an invisible string. He loved to move his body in abrupt angular patterns on the court to trick defenders. He would stop and go, stop and go, and his herky-jerky style frustrated opponents. They would sag off of C.J. and dare him to shoot, at which point he would smile, calmly step to the three-point line and fire the ball with either hand. More often than not, his shot was "money," as he used to say.

What C.J. loved most about basketball was the freedom to move uninhibited across the court, to use his quickness and speed to reach any spot on the floor. Pushing the ball between his legs, dancing from one angle to the next, seeing how fast he could execute each dribble move—it was soothing. Once he reached his sweet spot, C.J. would glide off his right foot with the ball in his left hand before finally switching it over to his right hand for a lay-up off the glass. Sometimes he would sprint to each hoop in the gym, scoring, then driving to the next basket to do it all over again. The predictable rhythm of dribbling the ball and scoring the hoop contrasted sharply with the instability of his life outside of basketball.

Watching C.J., who was a few years younger than me, dribbling down the court and scoring baskets, I had no idea that he would end up in prison just like his father; that he would become a crack dealer and gunshot survivor. The night we met in front of Marvin's old apartment, the trauma of his past oozed from his skin. His body looked dry and beaten, his eyes were sunken in and hollow. Dark bags hung beneath his eyelids; his lips were cracked black from the stain of marijuana smoke. A noticeable glimmer of light, however, remained in his eyes.

"Standing before the judge," C.J. later explained. "I'll never forget. He called me a wounded fox. He said that I was acting out like a hurt fox. He told me that before he gave me eighteen months in prison." "How did it get to that point?" I asked. "How did you go from running up and down the court in the neighborhood to standing before a judge who gave you an eighteen-month sentence?" "The struggle life," C.J. responded. "Almost everyone I ever cared for died." C.J. had been carrying around all those dead bodies, and their weight just became too heavy to bear. I knew then that my grieving for and rekindling of Marvin's spirit in the woods might become relevant for C.J.'s own journey. If a second life were possible for C.J., I thought, eventually he would have to confront the pain of losing so many loved ones.

THE TOLL OF VIOLENCE AND DEATH

The first person C.J. ever lost was his father. Although initially, the man wasn't physically dead, he had passed from C.J.'s life when he was locked up. C.J. found surrogate fathers at local basketball courts, many of whom showed him discipline and love. First there was Big Al, a towering man with a grainy voice and an extra dose of tough love. Big Al was strong. He did one hundred push-ups each morning before coaching kids. He was beloved, especially by those young men who did not have fathers at home. "Come on, C.J., get into it!" Al barked when he noticed C.J. jogging up the court. "Push the ball! Go!" C.J. would respond by crouching his body low to the ground and taking off at full speed with the ball like an Olympic sprinter. Coach Al would let out his signature laugh and smile when he saw C.J. respond with such ferocity.

"Get real son!" Coach Barry would scream in his Caribbean accent at C.J. and me if we missed easy layups. Coach Barry was stricter than Big Al. "That ain't reaaaaal boooooy!" Barry boomed each time the ball clanged off the basket. But most of us ball players loved Coach Barry and found him comical. Sometimes we missed layups just to hear his signature lines. Then on our way home from the gym, if one of us did something stupid, we'd yell, "That ain't real boy! You better get real son!" and bust out laughing.

Of all our coaches, however, Coach Manny Wilson was our hero. Coach Manny, the first to teach C.J. or me basketball, was like a superman with special powers. He was six-feet-four-inches tall, carried a gun during the day as a Boston police officer, and sported boulders for biceps, calf muscles of steel, and pecs made out of iron. One time I remember Manny calling me over to the bench-press station in at the Yawkey Club weight room. "Come here, boy. Check this out." Manny flexed his forearm. His bicep swelled into an oversized apple. "Go ahead, touch it," he said. When I poked his flesh with my right index finger it felt like I hit a rock. Manny opened the gym for us every Saturday morning for a two-hour basketball practice and drove us home during the week if we played games late at night.

"Take that hat off in the gym and give me twenty," Manny would yell whenever C.J. entered the gym with his hat on. C.J. would drop to the floor and count out twenty push-ups. "One, two." "Don't go down for the next push-up until I say down," Manny would demand. "Hold it there." Manny would make C.J. sweat for that last push-up. "Nineteen . . . Nineteen . . . Nineteen . . . Down . . . Twenty!"

Manny also taught us how to play basketball together as a team. We ran a two-three zone defense, with two guards rushing the other team's point guard at half-court. We played a one-three-one motion offense, guards passing to the wing and screening away, big men moving between the free-throw line and the low post. When we felt anxious during games, Manny knew instantly to call a time-out. "Okay, are you ready to play now? You got the nerves out?" "Yes," we would respond collectively. "Okay, than get your hands in." Our hands in the center, we yelled: "One, Two, Three, hard work!" in unison.

C.J. was ten years old when Manny died. Back then I never had a chance to speak to him about Manny's death. The car accident occurred a block away from Marvin's old apartment, where I would be reunited with C.J. years later. C.J. had lost another father. "I got my strength, some of my strengths come from Manny," he explained.

I just remember him like just pulling people off the streets to come in and play basketball. It is still unbelievable that he passed you know? All I remember hearing is that he was in the car wreck and that he was gone, but it is like he's still here somewhere you know? He's definitely still here through the basketball league, the Manny Wilson League that we played in, just everything, he was just a big dude. He was strong so that it's like I got my strength, some of my strengths come from Manny. He was the first dude that really put us in there, put me in there, because, um, it's still hard to believe that he's gone, 'cause really he's not gone. His spirit's gone but the whole Manny Wilson movement is still here. It's still here.

C.J.'s mother enrolled him in a predominately white elementary school soon after Manny's death. During school days, C.J. was able to escape Roxbury's streets. The arrangement would have been beneficial had it not been for the racism he experienced in the suburbs. Some white students referred to him as a "nigger" when he arrived on campus. To be called a "nigger" confused and robbed C.J. of his identity. He knew that the word signified his people's enslavement and dehumanization at the hands of whites. He desperately searched for a word that could hurt whites just as much, but their ancestors had not been enslaved and many knew the origins of their progenitors. Since no shield or sword could be found in the English language, he turned to his fists instead.

Racism played a part in my life at an early age. Going to a Janesbe school, about fourteen minorities on the bus going to a predominately white school in Janesbe. A couple of years I was the only African American kid in the class, you know?

I had a couple of kids, you know, they called me out my names and I dealt with them you know? I dealt with them sometime, but after a while I lost my cool because I never, I couldn't, I never had a name to call them back that matched the names that they would call me you know? And they would get away with it because you know, I was a, like I said, there was only a few minorities going to school and I was like one of the darker shade ones there, so if I was to put my hands on somebody for hurting my feelings, I would get in trouble for it or they would tell them "oh, I didn't say that" [C.J. speaks

with a wimpy "white" voice]. So, you know, I ended up getting
kicked out of the school, you know?

As we spoke, it became obvious that C.J. was still haunted by the injury
of going nameless in the minds of other people.[2] He did attempt to
turn the word "nigger" around on the white boys who were unaware
that its dictionary definition was "ignorant person." By stripping the
term of its racial meaning, C.J. tried to remove its sting. It was ironic
to him that those who referred to blacks as "niggers" were actually
"niggers" themselves. His ability to signify on his oppressors through
the use of irony helped him cope with the tragedy of his situation.

It was definitely a race thing. Because you know, when you got
people using the word "nigger" and they don't know the definition of it to call you "nigger" and especially if they're a Caucasian person or another race outside the African American
race you take it personally you know? Because if you tell them
to define it, they know the definition is ignorant person, but
they're not going to tell you "I'm calling you a nigger because
you're ignorant." So you get it from all angles and you know, I
mean, I dealt with it then, but it's helping me now because you
know, being, seeing certain situations and still hearing things,
racism going on now, prejudice and all that.
  Recently when I was incarcerated I heard, um, a Caucasian
person call somebody a "nigger." Now me in elementary, I
would have beat the person up, or we would have been fighting. But me now, knowing that the true definition to the word
is always going to be an ignorant person, I just, I never even, I
just washed it away. I didn't tell the person. I just kept it moving because for somebody to call, whatever race it is, for somebody to call and use that name, that word, they are themselves
an ignorant person because it's a substitute word for ignorant

so instead of you using words like that, you can just call a person, "yo, you're ignorant." You know, "yo, you're an ignorant
person," you know? So, I mean, I dealt with it but basketball,
you know, it makes up for that because like I said, my best
friend was a Caucasian person and I played with everybody,
you know? I played with everybody.

Given his early experiences with racism, it may be surprising to
hear that C.J.'s childhood best friend was white. He crossed over
racial lines on suburban basketball courts too. During the school
year, C.J. would collect his Roxbury friends and "barnstorm" the
suburbs to play against white players. They would ride on "white"
subway routes, where commuters stared suspiciously at their hoodies, Timberland boots, and gym bags. C.J. and his black friends
assumed stereotypes about whites as well, believing that white
ballplayers were "pure" jump shooters. "They got jump shots," C.J.
would tell his black friends as they rode the train.

I actually, now there's a new thing going on now where you'll
see a group of kids. You'll see them at downtown crossing
where you can get on the red line, the green line and they got
their Champion hoodies on, their skullies, their Tims and
today's stereotype is "oh, they out here, selling drugs, with
guns and stuff like that, especially with the book bags on." But
actually they have sneakers in their bags with a basketball, and
they going out to Chelsea somewhere, South Boston, from
Roxbury, to go play basketball. I mean, me, myself and I, I
use to travel, 'cause I use to go to school in Janesbe. I went to
Memorial Janesbe Elementary school there and my best friend
was a white person, a Caucasian person.

His name was Amos Ferrel, and the funny thing is I live
on Maybury Street in Roxbury. He lives on Maybury Street
in Janesbe. I bumped into a lot of basketball courts out there.

There were a few kids, you know, with nice jump shots out there [laughs], so I had to bring the best defenders out there for that, you know? [laughs] I use to tell 'em "listen these boys got some jump shots out there. We got the dribble but they got the jump shots." So we would round up and get on the bus and go play basketball.

C.J. is still trying to find his best friend Amos. They were separated on the day C.J. was expelled from Janesbe Memorial School for punching a white student in the face for calling him a "nigger." "Onaje," he said, "I have to find Amos one day. If I ever get to tell my story, I want Amos to be there in the audience."

A white administrator looked C.J. directly in the face on the day he was expelled and told him, "You don't deserve to be here." He felt as though she derived satisfaction from seeing him in pain. Years later, he bumped into her at a park in Roxbury. She was volunteering at an all-black lacrosse camp. "C.J., I'm so sorry for what I did to you," she pleaded. "I'm here today to try and make up for how I treated you kids." He didn't pay her apology much mind. He was thankful, but it was far too late.

After his expulsion C.J. returned to the pop of gunshots and screaming sirens in his Roxbury neighborhood. He played basketball often to avoid gangs and street violence. Basketball was a raft that kept him afloat in a sea of hopelessness.

Keep playing because I have, it was either play basketball or be in the house or just be around the way doing nothing and just watching the police fly up and down the street, hearing the shots or things that I didn't want to be involved in but when it came to going to the boys and girls club I knew there was a basketball and a hoop, and I knew there was somebody that was going to be in front of me and I'd be able to crossover and just go to the hoop and score. I can go hard you know?

Without basketball, man, my life could have been different in a million ways. Without basketball, I know for sure without basketball I wouldn't be here right now because it took a lot of extra time out of my life, extra time that I would have had to have been caught up in drugs, violence, walking across the street while there was a police chase, getting hit by a car, you know, getting hit by a stray bullet you know, just a lot of pain, you know, because while the whistle is blowing on the court and you're out there playing, you're spending maybe two to five hours a day playing basketball hard. Within those two to five hours I was playing basketball I know for sure at least, the way Boston was going, at least two people were dying in the area, or people were getting locked up. Things were happening! Houses were getting, I know my house got robbed once and I was at the boys and girls club playing basketball at the time, you know? I could have been in the house while that was happening and people just took me hostage or killed me because I was there and witnessed what they were doing. So basketball definitely saved me in a million ways, I know.

C.J.'s cousin, Eric Paulding, the one whose face, along with Marvin Barros Jr.'s, adorns the Community Awareness Tournament banner, had not been so fortunate. C.J. and Eric had been inseparable. The two were so close that C.J. wrote a story about him for his elementary teacher. In fact, on the day Eric was murdered, in 1997, he and C.J. were scheduled to meet. As C.J. gathered his belongings and put the finishing touches on his outfit, the words "first teen in 29 months slain in Boston," flew across the television screen. Then flashed the name "Eric Paulding." C.J couldn't believe his eyes and continued to dress as he saw a lifeless body roll across the screen on a stretcher. His aunt confirmed the tragic news. C.J. had lost another loved one.

C.J. had lost his father to prison when he was seven; coach Manny Wilson died when he was ten. He had been expelled from school largely due to racial violence, and now Eric had been murdered. After that, he just stopped caring since people died anyway. What was the point of life? Violence, a foreshortened future, death—that was all that made sense. The gritty logic of the streets made its way into his consciousness. He considered becoming a "street person" rather than a ballplayer, and these two poles of his identity were now at war inside of him. The day after Eric was murdered, C.J. had a basketball game. He woke up early with his dead cousin on his mind and although he was angry, he also knew that Eric would have wanted him to play the game. So he decided to put on his shorts and head down to the court.

"MY COUSIN WAS THERE WITH ME STILL"

During pregame warm-ups C.J. put his "sad face on." He shot the basketball with his cousin in mind. Normally he would push the ball rapidly between his right and left hands before driving into the lane for a finger-roll lay-up. But now he was lethargic with the ball in his hands. He had no desire to be in control anymore. Control was pointless and too painful. Strangely enough, however, C.J. couldn't miss a shot, and no one could steal the ball from his hands. Normally, when he performed his quick dribble moves, slapping the ball rapidly to the floor at impossible angles, he could make a mistake. But now the ball took on the personality of a loyal friend. When he pushed the ball toward the rim, it followed. When his palm guided the ball gently to the ground it hit the floor smoothly before rising to a perfect height. Feeling the synchronicity between his body and the basketball, C.J. explained, "My cousin was there with me still." His cousin had taken over the game just when C.J. had no desire to.

As I spoke with C.J., he explained that his need to rework life's problems by playing basketball was not uncommon for black boys in the city. Street-ball players, he said, use the game to "take them there"—to take their minds to another place and time. Their game is good, he went on, because their lives are bad. When Eric died, C.J. gave his heart on the asphalt.

Ah, man, playing. I can remember playing one day. I had a game. My cousin, he had passed away, my favorite cousin you know? I wrote a book about him when I was younger and he had got shot and he had passed away and I was down. I was down and I was miserable, but I was like "what am I going to do? I got a game today." So I went to the game.

I mean it's funny because I'm not going to say I didn't want to play. I still wanted to play basketball, but I had that on my mind. You know, and that was serious, you know? Because most people, something like that would have happened they wouldn't even go to a game, but I still had love for the game and before he passed I know he had love for the game too. So I go into the game, I had the sad face on and I don't know what it was you know? I just played and I know I wasn't playing as hard as I use to play, but everything was just, everything was going in man, everything. And I wasn't shooting the ball hard as I used to, dribbling it hard but I never got stripped. I don't know why. Usually somebody just come take the ball right out of my hand but it was just the love of the game I had and I believe my cousin was there with me still.

And there's so much people go through when they're playing in the city. You know, there's people who come to the game and they're alright you know? They had a good day, a good regular day but they come to play. But there's people, you know, they come on the court, they have issues you know? Some people, they done been through some things but they know basketball is going to take them there, you know, take their mind off of it. And for the most part I seen people, like, they just came from the streets, something happened, or something happen in the house and they're putting up forty, fifty points, like letting it all out, you know? Like dag, what happened to you today, you know?

So just life man, like that's why you have so many tough players in the city right now because man, they done been through some things man and everything's not good. There game is good, because of the things they done been through, the struggle, you know and just life itself. It's not that easy, so that's why, they put their heart on the court you know?[3]

C.J.'s attempt to make peace with the death of his cousin on the basketball court was a powerful ritual, but its effects were short lived. No one was there to acknowledge his ordeal, and he swirled into a spiral of despair. He began smoking marijuana incessantly to numb the pain, which got him expelled again, this time from an inner-city school. In fact, school administrators reported him to the police. A few days later he was arrested and assigned a court date where he could be placed in a juvenile detention center. Eventually, C.J.'s mother was offered an excruciating choice: leave C.J.'s fate to the hands of the criminal justice system or send him to an all-black private school in Virginia known for offering troubled youth a second chance. His mother chose Horace Prep. C.J. was cautiously optimistic. He could escape prison to play ball, but he couldn't run from the memory of his cousin's murder. Upon his arrival in Virginia, C.J. immediately joined the basketball team and tried to focus on his studies. However, he still felt angry and sad inside, and lacking purpose, he began to frequent Virginia nightclubs where there were local gang members and drugs. The light of basketball slowly flickered out of his life.

You know, I went down there. It was a different experience because it was away from home. I'm on campus. I mean, but I still had things on my mind, but I was down there playing ball you know? I was playing ball and things but now it was easier.

I went because my cousin passed away. I just wasn't acting right after that. I wasn't acting right. I didn't care about a lot of things. I stopped going to school. I started getting involved with drugs, selling drugs, so my mother helped me. She, um, got me out of here. So she sent me down there. As time went by I got involved with going to clubs out there and the same type of things that was going on when I was here, was going on out there. I stayed away from it for a while, because, you know, I was meeting new people, you know, people from New York that I was playing basketball with, things like that. But when things didn't go right, it was easier for me to lean back to the street life, the easy street life. I lost effort, and you know, focus. I still played basketball, though. But you know I had drugs in my life, you know? I was smoking weed. I was even smoking cigarettes playing basketball. Unbelievable, but you know, um, I just stopped playing organized basketball, that's what happened, and just started being in the streets.

In 2000, I'm still down there. I come back home on vacation, but I'm still going to school. It's my last year. I'm not a basketball player anymore. I'm a street person, you know? I'm from the hood. I'm street now and I'm out there, you know, like I said, with the weed, selling drugs, you know, the guns. I was into that, you know? What happen was, uh, one day I came and I was looking for my friend, dude I met down there. I knocked on his door and asked for him, like "is he here?" His sister just looked at me and she just like, started crying and you know? Come to find out that he had got killed down there, you know?

Eventually C.J. learned that as his friend's body lay full of bullet holes, still shaking in the streets, police officers had stood by and simply watched. He was angry with the police but scared of the people who murdered his friend. He knew that rival drug dealers had killed his friend because they perceived C.J. and him to be their competition. He wondered if it was a mistake to choose the streets over basketball, but he felt like he had gotten too deep into the drug game. "You can't have one foot in, and one foot out, you know?"

Soon thereafter, C.J. received a call from the dealers who had murdered his friend, demanding a meeting. Reluctantly, he went, knowing "something bad was going to happen." When C.J. refused their request for him to sell drugs on consignment, gunshots rang out: "Pow! Pow! Pow!" One bullet tore through his arm; another grazed his head. He jumped in his car, bleeding, speeding from the scene straight to the hospital. He gave the surgeon a fake name to conceal the incident from Horace Prep. He was released the next morning; his arm was swollen where the staples fastened his ripped skin together.

PLAYING SHOT

C.J. did not want to raise any suspicions, so he returned to the basketball court where he had a game scheduled that afternoon with his team at Horace Prep. During the pregame warm-ups, he hid out in the locker room, carefully placing the uniform over his thick chest, slipping on his long dangling shorts and his size-nine sneakers. He checked the gaping hole in his arm and slipped a white athletic band over the torn skin. He exited the locker room and stepped onto the shiny hardwood floor.

During warm-ups no one noticed C.J.'s injury. When the pregame buzzer sounded, he huddled up with his teammates, keeping his left arm hidden from his coach. When the huddle broke away C.J. jogged to the half-court circle, crouched down and waited for the referee to throw the ball between the centers.

C.J. dribbled masterfully at first with his right hand. His ambidexterity was paying off, but as the game became more intense and unpredictable, he found it harder to hide playing shot. Anytime the ball rolled to his left side, he had to turn his body and dribble with his right. It seemed strange and unnatural for C.J. to avoid using his left hand, which was more dominant. "What's all this right-handed business?" the coach screamed from the sidelines. Staring at his coach, he finally blurted out: "I was hurt yesterday. I . . . I was shot." He was removed from the game quickly and escorted out of the gym. He confessed everything—getting shot, giving a false name to the surgeon, trying to cover up the injury on the court. Horace Prep sent C.J. back north, his third expulsion in less than eight years.

C.J.'s father died in prison shortly after he returned to Boston.

I had a lot of weight on me and I just came back. I definitely didn't have any . . . I didn't want to do anything. I just wanted to, whatever, I'm breathing, fine, you know? It was like, so much anger. I was still dealing with the guns, drugs, and things like that. And um, brought that attitude back man, and how Boston is here, it was like a great thing. It was a mixture, you know? Going to the parties here getting drunk and every-body's deep, you know hoodies and you know, they got their guns and you got your guns and it's just life man, you know, but honestly inside I didn't really want to be that way you know, but it was just a thing like, I lost all my turns. It was like a one-way alley right now. All my left, rights and I forgot how to take you know, my left turns and things, you know? It's like my steering car was broke, you know? I could only go straight down the one-way dead end, you know?

In 2000 he was arrested for selling drugs. Shortly thereafter he was pulled over for possession of a stolen motorcycle, drugs, and an illegal firearm. During that time he lost other friends. To numb the pain, he ingested more drugs.

Finally C.J. was sentenced to prison by the judge who referred to him as a "wounded fox." This particular judge had been aware that C.J.'s father had died in prison, and he attributed C.J.'s behavior to losing his father. Nevertheless, the sentence was for serious jail time. C.J. entered prison for the first time and discovered that the penitentiary was a microcosm of the streets. Violence earned respect, drugs could be sold for money, and gangs defined the rules of the game. In prison, he was taught to revel in crime. "I lost a lot of people so you know? It was my first time doing time, and I really didn't learn the right things when I went in there. I didn't know the rules of who to be around. I basically based myself around people who had fun with places like that. So I was having fun. I was having more fun than learning anything."

After eighteen months he returned to the streets, more lost than ever. Three weeks on the outside and he was arrested again, this time for armed robbery. Although there may have been some police misconduct in the case, he returned to prison for another fifteen months. This time in prison, however, C.J. began to reexamine his life, to try to understand how he had ended up in jail. He also returned to the asphalt courts inside the prison yard. He was short and had never been able to dunk, but all his pent up frustration and anger propelled him above the rim in jail. He dunked for the first time in prison, and he expressed his frustration by putting up insane points each game during rec time. Jail ball became such a critical part of C.J.'s mental health that he begged other inmates to avoid confrontations with correction officers before rec period. Rec time delays meant less time on the court, and prison games started and ended when correction officers said they did. During his last few months in jail, he slowly began to envision other possibilities for his life. He still carried around the heavy memories of lost loved ones, but now there was hope.

Ah, man! You couldn't believe some of the people they have in there playing ball. Like, you look at them and you like, dag, why aren't you on the screen right now, you know? I mean they're dunking on you, they're crossing over, their jump shot is just natural and people got game. You know it's just, they channel their anger and their frustration the wrong ways but they just need a little bit of guidance and help, but for me it was like, whoa! I can tell you right now that I was in there. I was dunking on people! I tell my boys all the time "like yo, I was in there. I was doing my thing! I was ballin' 'em up! I had forty something!" And they're like, "yeah, whatever!" you know, but I had that basketball in there and all my frustration went out on the court and I did things that people looking at me to this day, people that I did time with, they're like, "yo, what's up, you in school yet?" You know, they're like, "yo, you better get back with the program man, you know?"

Um, definitely I let it all out on the court. I definitely had my time and that was one of the things that helped me learn things while I was in there because I had my basketball. I showed myself that I still got it. Like, my whole momentum, my attitude right now, is running off of basketball because I always said "I'm going to make it, I'm going to make it!" and right now I'm still feeling like I'm going to make it just because I know I can get on the court today and do somebody in on the court so that keeps me going knowing that however, I'm going to make it one day. And if I can get back on track and get into school, I know I'm going to get that basketball fever back. So one way or another I'm going to make it through the basketball you know?

Once C.J. was released from prison the second time, he had begun to turn his life around. He began playing basketball again and even rented an apartment with a girlfriend to solidify their relationship. He was still being followed by police officers. Occasionally, they would bust open his apartment door unannounced in search of weapons and drugs. It bothered him, but as long as they didn't plant evidence, he wasn't going back to jail.

A few days after his release from prison we had spotted each other at the crossroads in front of Marvin's old house. He had already seen so much struggle and death, and as he later explained, basketball was his hope for a "second life."

Things I have been experiencing from since I was younger till now, just struggle life, but how to maintain the struggle life. How to keep my composure, make it through rough times, you know, just you know, wealth-wise, street-wise.

The only thing I really been winning in so far is basketball if I think about it. Life has been a struggle. I'm a call it losing you know, 'cause it's an everyday struggle, you know. People need basketball. It's like . . . it's life itself, it's a part of life, it's a second life to people.

"How can you achieve a second life through basketball after all you've been through?" I once asked C.J. He wasn't sure. All he knew was that his undoing began with his cousin's murder. He explained that if he could just go back to that moment in time in his own consciousness, then maybe he could see how he had gone wrong, why he had lived like a wounded fox for all those years. "Maybe if you had fully grieved that day," I suggested. "Maybe if someone had acknowledged your pain, maybe eventually you would have been able to let him go instead of carrying him around all those years." "Yeah," C.J. said. "I did that once in prison. I went back in time to my cousin's murder, but I never fully got there." "Maybe that's the only way for you to achieve a second chance at life," I said. "To face death." "Yeah, maybe," he responded.

Since that day we reunited in the middle of the road, C.J. and I have remained close. I introduced him to Jason, and the three of us played city basketball together. As I thought about C.J.'s story, I wondered whether street basketball could ever be more than a tool of survival for young black men. Could hope ever lead to healing? In the last two chapters, I take up the question of whether the "lived religion" of street basketball can restore a sense of wholeness in the lives of some young black men and their communities.

PART 3

HEALING

5

ANCESTOR WORK IN STREET BASKETBALL

The spirit of the dead must live its life one more time in an accelerated fashion before departing to the realm of the ancestors. . . . It is believed that doing what was once done frees the living from the dead and vice versa.

—Malidoma Patrice Some, *Ritual*

I had just attended the 2013 Community Awareness Tournament in Roxbury. It was dark. I walked aimlessly along St. Mary's Street near Boston University. Painful images of the young boys and men of Roxbury flooded my head. That afternoon Russell had asked me to read Marvin's "Let It Be Magic" poem at halftime to the crowd. I couldn't do it. Grief racked my body. I left the game. Tears rolled down my eyes as the full impact of the interviews and stories of Boston's black young men hit me. This wasn't a few suffering individuals—it was a collective injury. I thought back to the metaphor of the three rings of the asphalt, the outer circle representing the violated black communal body. Take Marlon, whom I mention in the introduction. He was a long and skinny six-foot-two-inch player from Roxbury, versatile as a Swiss army knife. He shot threes from deep, made defenders fall with his hesitation dribble, and dunked on players off of one leg. A rhythmic beat reverberated through his head and the sound would grip his body during games:

> It seemed like I always had a song going in my head, but I never knew what the song was. That's just how my game was. It felt like I was dancing on the court. It's not trying to show off, it's just how my mind was going and obviously achieved. My mind had a song and I'm bumping to it in my head so now on the court it got me—I'm about to go dunk on somebody or I'm about to go shoot somebody's lights out. I'm about to cross somebody. It was funny, it's like I don't know how many dudes that I made fall just from a simple move. Not even a crossover. A quick step and like "see you later." Go down, roll it, dunk it.

Marlon, however, was almost raped by his abusive stepfather in a pissy Boston housing project building as a child. Fortunately, he fought him off, dressed his little sister, and hustled down several miles of snow-filled sidewalks to his grandmother's apartment. His biological father was in prison and his mother was a drug addict, like so many parents of other ballplayers that I interviewed. "I'd run into somebody that was always like, 'Your mom just copped [bought] some morphine,' " explained Marlon. "I tell them, don't sell nothing to my mom. I'll kill you. That's what I tell a person. It's like, 'little nigger get the fuck out of here. You ain't got no gun.' 'Oh, I don't. Okay, be right back.' [I'd] walk right into the projects. Saw one of the older dudes that know my mother and know my father like, 'yo' such and such this and such and such is my mom's.' 'Here take that . . .' " and the older gangster would hand him a gun.

Marlon's mother was his biggest fan before she contracted HIV and died. After her death, he was so grief-stricken that he stopped playing altogether. He turned to marijuana and alcohol to keep the pain at bay. After bingeing on drugs one night and falling asleep, he dreamed of his mother, who told him:

> "Put that [alcohol] shit down. Get your shit together and get on that court." So that following year, sophomore year, came I balled all on out. Made it all the way. Only sophomore on the team playing with nothing but juniors and seniors. Played with one of the street-ball legends . . . Jay . . . He was on my team. . . . Yeah, she told me to get my shit together. I jumped out of my sleep sweating and crying.

Marlon's dream was a wake-up call. He returned to the basketball court, even though heartbroken. Tears rolled down my face as I thought about Marlon, imagining him running in the snow, sister in arms, fleeing a rapist, mother dead, HIV, playing hoops in order to keep a small part of himself alive. I peered down St. Mary's hill to Boston University's Martin Luther King Jr. memorial. The doves of peace atop the statue were lit up as if ascending toward the sky. Even so, I only felt hopelessness thinking about young black men in exile in the dark of the night. I thought about Jamal, a young African American ball player whose mother was fourteen when she gave birth to him. The grandparents who raised him were crack addicts. He didn't really know his father. Jamal went to the basketball court to express the pain he experienced at home and to bond with guys who shared similar stories. Being on the asphalt meant he didn't have to carry the burden of his family's struggles alone. "[Basketball] was a getaway, it was a means to just to get away from all the stuff that was going in my household, and when you're around a bunch of kids, peers your age that are going through the same thing that love this game the same way. They found at this young age that we could express our self in there."

Jamal's grandfather was his greatest male role model, especially when he finally quit using narcotics. In fact, Jamal's whole family became drug-free by the time he reached high school, and they were thrilled when Jamal was selected to play basketball for a predominately white and affluent prep school in Connecticut. On Thanksgiving Day, however, as Jamal prepared for a basketball game, his beloved grandfather passed away. "That was a big loss," he reflected. "That was like the last or the only father figure I had at that time that would push me."

During the game with his team at Dupont Prep, Jamal intended to mourn the loss of his grandfather on the basketball court. However, he was far away from home and his coaches, fans, and other players could not understand how he was using basketball to vent his frustrations and sorrow. In the midst of his sense of isolation, all of his shots careened off the rim, and he interpreted the missed goals as a sign of the ritual's failure. Soon after the game, he rejected basketball and spirituality altogether, eventually turning to drugs:

> It was horrible, I might have went oh for fifteen. I had a horrible game. . . .
>
> I couldn't even focus on the game honestly it was just more so I just kept thinking about [my grandfather].
>
> During the game, crying at halftime like I couldn't even . . . I thought I could deal with it but I really couldn't, and I thought I could go out here and this would be a means for me to get away from that. But I couldn't and that was a real tough time.
>
> I'm at a prep school so I'm around a lot of people that don't really truly understand how we actually really like live honestly, honest like truly live. I'm talking about I'm at school with the Duponts and the real prestigious families. They honestly had no clue whatsoever how we was living.
>
> And it's crazy because after I lost my grandfather I was done with church and done with all that, I buried that. And it

got to a point where I didn't care about ball, I started to abuse marijuana more, I started to hang with gang members more. I started doing all the negativity.

Images of Jamal playing basketball for his beloved grandfather flowed through my mind. Much like C.J., he had not been able to really mourn. I wondered what would eventually happen in Jamal's life, and in the life of his children, if he never got to reconcile his relationship with his grandfather.

Baron, my informant, was another ballplayer who had been acquainted with far too much violence and death. In fact, he came close to dying himself. Ever since he was a child Baron had taken out all his anger on the basketball court:

My thing is, I don't think I ever really let out childhood anger except but on the court. It definitely gave me an out-let, because when you are eight to thirteen you fight on the street, you fight in school, you fight on the court, whatever, you get in trouble. In basketball you don't get in trouble. You can punch somebody's ball, yell. You can steal the ball, run, get tired, box out, get rebounds, use all these different type of tactics to make your opponent feel like, this kid's a problem, this kid's a beast. He might not be able to shoot, he might not be able to jump, but he's a headache on the rebounds. He just doesn't let up. He doesn't quit. So by the end of the game my own mind is, by the second quarter, four or five minutes left in the second half, if I'm tired, you're dirt tired. That's how I felt. If I get a little bit tired, I'm looking at my opponent like, if I'm tired, he's dead tired.

Baron's mother was also a crack addict, and his father was a ran-dom guy he passed by on the street once in a while. Sometimes they said "hello." He hated the Department of Social Services group homes he attended. Psychiatrists there would pump his body with pharmaceutical drugs to suppress his anger.

DSS programs try to use a drug to calm you down . . . like lithium, zipamine, repamine. These are all the different drugs they say calm you down, make sure you're relaxed for the day. None of that stuff ever works. If you going to fight you going to fight regardless. A drug can't tell you, it's not going to make you not fight. So it got to a point where they was like, we can't do nothing with him. So they pretty much kicked me out.

The day Baron was almost killed he was trying to protect his sister, who had been living in a violent area on Akron Street:

I mean you had like three different gangs up and down Akron. So all I knew is once one gun shot went off everyone started shooting, everyone! It didn't matter. Um, there was a kid in a wheelchair, he had guns! It was like I knew everybody out there. Everybody out there. It was crazy. I had nothing to do with it. Nothing to do with it at all.

I ended up being shot five times, in the neck, twice in my back, in the butt and in my leg. I kind of ran through it to get to my house because I was on the opposite side of the street, and I ran through it to get my sister off the porch. When I got in the house, in the hallway there was just blood everywhere and I thought it was her, so when I got up I'm like, "yo, you're bleeding!" She's like, "it's not me, it's you!" And once I noticed it [snaps his fingers] it's like you can feel it now, the sting, burning! Still didn't drop, but now I'm feeling my neck 'cause my neck is on fire! I'm feeling both sides of my back, the one in my leg kind of, it grazed me more than hit me, so I wasn't really worried but I'm feeling my neck, like something's wrong! And now I'm leaking with blood! I just dropped. The next time I woke up I was in the hospital.

Baron eventually recovered from his wounds in the hospital, but his brush with death changed his personality. He was angry all of the time, always two seconds away from exploding. Baron has lost several friends and family to death—so many, he stopped counting. But one stands out, a young man named Ty, whom Baron calls his "little brother." Ty was one of the few ball players who made it out of Roxbury and into college. Then one day, right on the hardwood, he just died. Baron was devastated.

That Thursday he played against one of my friends from the projects, Bobby. And I get a phone call from Bobby after their game. "Um, you know Ty passed out on the court. I think he's alright. They took him to the hospital. I'll call you later." So when I called him back he was like, "yeah man, he passed out man." So I kind of froze like, "is he alright?" "I don't know. I don't know. I don't know." I hung up the phone with him. He said his coach called a meeting with all the players or whatever. He said he would call me back.

Once I hung up the phone with him, Desmond called me. And everyone knew that me and Ty were like big brother, little brother. I looked at him more than a little brother than a lot of people in my family. Desmond called me and said, "I'm sorry to tell you this but Ty just died." And I said, "D, don't tell me that because Bobby told me he was alright." Sure enough the phone beeps and it's Bobby on the other line crying, and he said that they pronounced him dead pretty much on the basketball court but he was dead at the hospital.

Baron decided to go to the basketball court on the day of the church funeral to honor Ty's memory. He designed the ritual himself: a walk with Ty's family members to the court, a moment of reflection, pictures of Ty's face on everyone's uniform, an outpouring of tears before stepping onto the court, interpreting his made baskets as a sign of Ty's approval.

The day of um, my little brother's funeral, Ty Jones, um, it was a Thursday, and we had a game . . . [sighs] I had about thirty that game. And I remember I got some T-shirts made up with his face on them. And right after the funeral a few people went out to eat. I think I went home and just relaxed. The game was like at seven o'clock. I went to the game with some of the members from his family, from his mother's side and some of my friends. . . .

And every, I mean I got his tattoo on my arm, his initials, every game I go to the game I kiss my tattoo before the game, after the game, during the game, and I pretty much live through that man. Because he was a person, he didn't bother nobody. He loved life. He loved family, he loved friends, he loved air! He loved the sun, he loved rain, everything! He just loved life! And to see someone like that go, it just put life in a whole different perspective as far as what are we really doing here? What's your purpose? He served a purpose by touching out to us and making sure that we seen somebody who actually came here for twenty-two years.

As I wandered down St. Mary's hill, the accumulation of these painful narratives became overwhelming. How was it possible that so many of Boston's young black men shared these experiences? I thought about my own unexpressed grief over the deaths of Marvin and Manny. I needed to cry, not just because of the premature death of loved ones but because I had to leave my neighborhood and culture behind in order to tell this story.

At least through basketball, I was slowly returning home. Remember G-Big, the chubby boy who first initiated me into street basketball when I was nine years old? C.J. called me up one day from Roxbury with G-Big standing next to him. "Oh, I have a surprise for you. Hold on." C.J. handed over his cell phone: "Oh, it's me, your boy G-Big! Did C.J. tell you?" "What?" I said excitedly, glad to hear G-Big's voice for the first time in fifteen years. "My baby's mother, she was murdered." "What? Oh, I am so sorry, man. So sorry," I responded, staring down at my cell phone. Our first conversation in years and those were his first words. G-Big's girlfriend had been shot with an AK-47 and died on the spot. We hung up quickly. I haven't dialed his number again.

G-Big's girlfriend was murdered near Jermaine's house. I ran into Jermaine at one of the Save R Streets Basketball Classics. When he learned that I was writing a book about basketball, he urged me to visit his apartment a few days later so that he could share his story. "Basketball is everything," he told me.

> It has been the tool to my life to make me who I am. Without it, I don't know if I would be who I am. I know that point blank. Without basketball, will Jermaine be Jermaine? Would I know as many people? Would I walk the same? Would I talk the same? No, I would be someone totally different. I don't know what I would have done. . . . But this is who I am and basketball has made my life. There has to be part chromosome in there [in his DNA] with some stripes on it somewhere or something.

I found out that as a child Jermaine lacked proper food to eat. His mother and father raised him in a "drug-infested environment," and when he was three years old, he had to run across Brook Avenue to steal food from the local store. One day a car slammed into

Jermaine's body, which is how the Department of Social Services discovered his home situation and placed him in the care of his grandmother. She meant everything to him during his early years.

Eventually Jermaine's father moved in with Jermaine and his grandmother. His father also brought along his new wife and her son after divorcing Jermaine's mother, who continued to abuse drugs. It was confusing and painful, but he turned to the basketball court, where he was free to be himself.

> It's like church. It's like going into that silent time when you are just down. Everything you want to do, everything that you can think of, you're just doing it and trying it. There is like there are no faults, it's just you and the two goals and these lines. So I just felt the feeling of freedom. Being able to do whatever I want to do and nobody is going to judge me. If I miss it or if I make it, no whistle is going to go off. So it's just freedom man, just straight freedom.

Jermaine had lost loved ones in the streets as well. After his mentor and basketball coach, Buddy Taylor, died suddenly, Jermaine decided to play in a game to honor his memory. However, when he arrived at the court, he realized that he was the youngest player on a team full of Buddy's older friends. Jermaine felt intimidated and self-conscious about the possibility that he might make a mistake on the court. He did not want Buddy's older friends to view his missteps on the court as a sign of disrespect to Buddy's memory.

But in fact all Buddy's friends were wrestling with how to honor his life and death through basketball. Some thought that Buddy deserved a perfect game and rattled with emotion; they tried to control the outcome of every play.

> That experience was very intense because I played with the guys. I knew Buddy growing up. He was one of my older

guys that I looked up to. And the guy that I played for, those were his friends. They were his legitimate hangout buddies right there to that day. And as soon as the ball went up and a couple fouls were called, it was so emotional. I want to tear up now just thinking about it because it was very, very emotional. There were dudes crying and screaming. The game was emotionally packed. I am going to tell you his friends; they were his high school buddies. As a matter of fact, they played twelve-and-under with this guy. That's how close they were. And just playing in the game was like, everybody wants to be the hero just for him. It was all for him. Everything was for him. We had to win this for him. We have to do this for him. And when they put me in I kind of like was, "man, I want to go in because I know him, but I want to do so well and I don't want to mess up. I don't want no one mad at me."

The guy that coached pulled us to the side and said, "listen, if you guys are going to play for him, then play for him. But don't go out there and embarrass yourself because you are trying to play too outside yourself. Just play within yourself and play for him." And we won one game and lost the next one, but it was a hard-fought victory . . . people were talking to him. "This is for you Buddy." And just, "miss you." It was crazy man. I want to say that it was so long ago, it was like ten years ago man. I can't believe that he's been gone that long. He has been gone that long.

As Commonwealth Avenue grew silent late into the night, an overwhelming sense of sadness weighed on me. The basketball court was obviously a place where young black men felt comfortable mourning death, but I still had so many unanswered questions. Did these grief rituals have a basic structure, and if so, what were its key elements? If young men were mourning on the court, why did their feelings of anger and violence not dissipate thereafter? Were crucial elements missing from their grieving practices, elements that kept black men from forgiving themselves and bearing no malice toward others?

"I COULD HAVE DIED AND WENT TO HEAVEN RIGHT THERE"

In an attempt to answer these questions, I examine NBA player Chris Paul's memorial game for his grandfather, "Papa Chilli," through the lens of ritual theory. Paul's grief ritual, which occurred soon after the loss of his grandfather, exposes the limitations of black men's grieving practices in Boston's inner city. It also represents an optimal model of healing for these young black men in the future.

Chris, a prolific point guard and president of the National Basketball Players Association, was born and raised in Lewisville, North Carolina, within a tightknit African American extended family. His immediate relatives included his parents, Robin and Charles Paul, and an older brother, C.J. Charles, C.J., and Chris all share the same initials, which is why Chris Paul is better known as CP3. Although Paul's immediate family offered him a safe haven as a child, there was no greater figure and mentor in CP3's life than his grandfather Nathaniel Jones. Papa Chilli was Chris's best friend and counselor on and off the court.

Nathaniel Jones was a pillar in Lewisville's black community. The state's first African American founder and owner of an automotive service station, he commanded respect. During times of hardship, extended family members and friends turned to Nathaniel, who always extended his support. Papa Chilli's grandsons adored him and could often be found by his side fixing cars. Papa Chilli was equally proud of his grandsons. He attended all of Chris's basketball games, demonstrating his undying love with his presence on the sidelines: "I felt my granddad was my biggest fan," Chris once said. "I would go out to the service station to see him and you know, he would just be, um, he would always be bragging on me and my brother about how good we were, and he just [pause] . . . he just made me feel different."[1] (I am reminded here of Jason's comments about his great-grandmother, who "put something into me," and the power of elders to bestow a feeling of worth on young people.)

Chris was much shorter than his older brother, C.J., during his early years. C.J was a hoops star, leading his West Forsyth High School basketball team before matriculating to Hampton University and the University of South Carolina Upstate, where he played college ball. Eventually, however, Chris caught up to his older brother in height and basketball talent. By the time he was a senior at West Forsyth, he averaged 25.0 points, 4.4 steals, and 5.3 assists a game, all while his doting grandfather cheered from the crowd.

Chris's impressive basketball skills made it almost a foregone conclusion that he would matriculate to nearby Wake Forest University, where his grandfather could continue to attend his games. When Chris signed his letter of intent to attend Wake Forest, Papa Chilli stood there right beside him, proudly placing a Wake cap on his grandson's head.

On the following day, however, five African American boys robbed, duct-taped, and beat Papa Chilli to death with metal pipes for the cash in his wallet. All five boys were close in age to Chris when they brutally ended Nathaniel Jones's life. Eventually, all five were arrested and convicted. Two are currently serving life sentences. The other three were sentenced to fourteen- and fifteen-year prison terms.

The Ritual Structure of Chris Paul's Memorial Game

The African scholar and shaman Malidoma Patrice Some suggests that rituals can be defined as any human attempt to communicate with spirit.[2] He argues that the structure of a ritual generally follows a tripartite form, which includes an opening, a dialogue, and a closing. Some's understanding of ritual as a three-stage process shares similarities with Arnold van Gennep's well-known stage theory of ritual, which involves the processes of separation, threshold, and aggregation.[3] The core assumption underlying both concepts is that rituals facilitate individuals and groups to move from one status or condition (separation) through a state of ambiguity (threshold) to a new way of being in the world (aggregation).

Some emphasizes the intermediate stage (dialogue) as ritual's most transformative dimension. During this phase, individuals place their previous assumptions about the world in abeyance and are able to recognize the historically constructed nature of their identities. For individuals and communities whose lives are largely determined by "symbolic violence," the capacity to displace the natural "order of things," can become critical for survival. The philosopher Dwayne Tunstall refers to this practice as an "ego-displacement technique" where persons of African descent bracket " 'the reality' of racial categories" in order "to 'see' the world as a racialized one."[4]

Tunstall suggests that these techniques derive their origins from the rituals of African traditional religions. Many practitioners of African traditional religions perform ritual "in order to prepare themselves for an examination of *how* their lived experiences are co-constituted by the relationships, encounters, and engagements she has with other living persons, her ancestors, other living organisms, and her environing world."[5] Tunstall points out that for these religious practitioners the human ego represents a necessarily limited and socially constructed version of the self and world. Ritual is therefore required to reclaim the self's authenticity and rootedness in its more spiritual ground.

Some shares Tunstall's views concerning the ego-transformative potential of ritual, arguing that ritual practice must be distinguished from ceremonial behavior on the basis of whether or not the ego dominates the activity. He suggests that while ceremony constitutes an ego-centered activity (which he defines as the repetitive structure or "anatomy" of ritual),[6] the essence of ritual is a spontaneous dialogue between humans and spirit. Though ceremony may effectively relate human beings to each other (often hierarchically), ritual connects persons to gods.

The Crisis of Death: Separation

Marginalized African American people in U.S. cities are continuously confronted with the crisis of death, which is bound to produce a sense of disorientation among the bereaved. Some suggests that this sense of inner turmoil is the first step toward ritual because it places the bereaved person into a state of doubt regarding the veracity of the world. Sigmund Freud framed this state of disorientation in the context of wishful thinking, as the bereaved person is prone to fantasize about a possible reunion with a lost loved one despite the fact that he or she is gone.[7] When Papa Chilli was murdered, Chris expressed an initial sense of disorientation and doubt: "We went to my granddad's house and I didn't want to believe it. And all I wanted to do when I got out the car was see my granddad and he wasn't there. I just [pause] . . . you know everybody has to die, but I just thought that my granddad was one of those people who never would, never would."[8]

Other scholars have been critical of Freud, however, for reducing the bereaved person's attachment to the deceased to a psychic fantasy.[9] Detractors have argued that a bereaved person's feelings of inner turmoil and emotional angst may also represent the lingering energetic presence of the deceased. Freud's view, in other words, only takes into account the experience of the bereaved person who is still physically alive. Some, by contrast, suggests that the spirit of the recently deceased is also disoriented, suddenly detached from its body and thrust into a state of limbo. This state of spiritual ambiguity among the deceased is what produces an analogous sense of turmoil for the living. Some reinterprets the bereaved person's felt sense of sorrow, anger, and fear as the dead ghost's restless energy. While Freud argued that the basic work of mourning is to free the mourner from these emotions, Some suggests that grieving also serves to release the spirit of the dead from its needless attachments to the physical world. Spirits who are not mourned properly become what Toni Morrison famously referred to in *Beloved* as the "the black and angry dead," winning the attention of the living by causing more heartache and destruction.[10] Some's spiritual interpretation of the mourning process makes an important contribution to the literature on the cycle of violence within urban black communities. In addition to the structural, institutional, and interpersonal causes of premature death, Some's work suggests that there is a deeper spiritual dimension of this collective injury. Some's spiritual perspective is also hopeful because it recognizes that a reunion between the living and the dead is not "wishful thinking." Instead, the living and the dead remain codependent even after the physical body has decayed. The act of grieving then may be understood as a radical act of liberation and healing, because once the spirits of the deceased are at peace, they are more likely to generate accord among the living.

Opening a Threshold Between Worlds

Some suggests that in order to open the threshold between worlds, the living must find some way to invoke the spiritual presence of the deceased. Invocations take many forms, some of which include prayers, gestures, dances, sounds, images, and thoughts. The key to invocations is that they must signify the intention of the bereaved person to dialogue with the deceased's spirit as part of the grieving process. During Boston's memorial games, for example, players placed images of deceased relatives on iron fences and walls around the basketball court. Others kissed tattoos right before crossing the lines that separated the court from their everyday lives in the neighborhood. Others simply contemplated memories of deceased loved ones as they took warm-up shots. Chris's memorial game was no different in this regard. He too, meditated on memories of Papa Chilli throughout the game. According to Some, these invocation techniques shift the energy of a ritual space (such as the basketball court), calling the spirit of the departed into the performance.

Another element involved in creating a ritual space, although not always available, is the active involvement of community elders. The conscious participation of elders is one of the most striking differences between Chris's grief ritual for his granddad and the mourning practices of Boston's young black men. Two days after Papa Chilli's death, Chris's aunt came to her nephew's side and suggested that he score a point for every year of his grandfather's life in his next high school basketball game. In that moment, she stood in her nephew's shoes and offered a creative response to his inner needs: "My first thought was: how can I go out there on the court, knowing that my grandfather's not there?" Chris wondered. "And my aunt mentioned before I went to the park and game, she said: 'How about sixty-one points for your granddad?' And I just thought to myself, you know that would be lovely. And I just thought to myself, ain't no way I could do that."[11]

The absence of a critical mass of elders (there are, of course, dedicated individuals) standing behind Boston's city hoops players is a symptom of the collective injury haunting these urban neighborhoods. More often than not, Boston's inner-city basketball players turn themselves into choreographers of the court, summoning the courage to mourn without witness. C.J., for instance, went to the court with his "sad face on." Baron designed T-shirts with Ty's face and broke down right before the game. When Shorty was released from prison, he made his own way to the asphalt to remember Kane.

Between Worlds: Dialoguing with Spirit on the Court

From Some's perspective, once a person has invoked spirit and left the familiarity of everyday life, dialogue with a spirit world becomes possible. In street basketball, the movement of player's bodies, the ball, and the hoop may turn into vocabularies of spiritual communication. Similar to the art of divination, throwing the ball up and down the court gives players access to a form of spiritual feedback. The frequency with which the ball enters the basket says something about the activity of the spiritual world. Chris described this back-and-forth dialogue with Papa Chilli: "This is one of the times that I just felt there's no way that, I don't care what kind of defense you play, who you put in front of me. There's no way you are going to stop me from getting to that goal. The whole game I was just think-ing about my granddad, just thinking, you know, he's in heaven, he's watching this game, he's watching this game. Every time somebody hits me to the floor, he's up there jumping out his seat getting angry. And as the course of the game went on, I said 'I can do this.' "[12]

Some suggests that employing one's own bodily movements as a spiritual metaphor is precisely what is required to "stimulate the grief catharsis" in the funerary rites of his Dagara community in Burkina Faso, West Africa. During the "dialogue" stage of tra-ditional Dagara funerals, friends and relatives reenact the deceased person's life.

Besides the xylophone, drumming and singing to stimulate the grief catharsis, there is another important part to the funeral ritual. The life of an adult who dies must be reen-acted by the surviving members of his initiation group. All the males who were initiated at the same time as the departed one will, in the second or third day, re-enact the person's life. That portion of the ritual is called *xanu*. It means dream, as if the dead were dreaming his life. The spirit of the dead must live its life one more time in an accelerated fashion before departing to the realm of the ancestors. . . . It is believed that doing what was once done frees the living from the dead and vice versa.[13]

There is remarkable parallelism between Some's description of a Dagara funerary reenactment and Chris's pledge to score a point for every year of his grandfather's life on the second day after his murder. At least on a symbolic level, each point represented his life in an "accelerated fashion." But Chris's description of his experience indicates that something occurred beyond mere symbolism. Toward the end of the game, after he had already scored fifty-nine points, Chris drove to the right side of the hoop, leaped into the air, and kissed the ball off the glass to score the sixty-first point. At that moment he collapsed onto the hardwood, his body seemingly limp and lifeless: "It felt like I could have just died and went to heaven right there. It felt like my purpose for being here was almost over."[14] It is difficult to know whom Chris is referring to at this point, himself or his grandfather.

Closing Ritual: Returning Home

Some suggests that once communication with spirit has ended, a ritual can be closed through an expression of gratitude. The act of thanking spirit closes the ritual because it tells the spirit that the purpose of the ritual has been achieved. Boston's street-basketball players expressed gratitude in different ways to signal the end of a grief ritual. Baron kissed his tattoo of Ty after games. Jason stood on the basketball court, as the mantra "thank you, thank you" washed over his whole body, in appreciation for his life. Unfortunately, however, it is also true that players are often unable to close the space of ritual because there is no one to welcome them back home. It was Jason's trainer who confirmed for him that his ordeal was actually over: "I started crying and when that trainer started, when I seen her crying that was honestly one of the best feelings in my life.... She truly, deeply understood ... she started crying the same way I started crying."

Boston's street-basketball players generally lack the witness of an elder who may affirm their special inner qualities after undertaking such an arduous ordeal. Some suggests that the absence of elders to close a ritual properly is dangerous because both humans and spirits remain unacknowledged, stuck in a perpetual state of turmoil and confusion. Chris, by contrast, scored his sixty-first point, intentionally missed a free throw, and walked over to the sidelines and into his father's arms. "I just looked at my Dad and started crying." His father confirmed: "It's just like everything came out of him. He just walked over to me and gave me a hug and just fell in my arms and that's when I just, it just tore me up, you know, 'cause of what he had just done."[15] The absence of elders to open and close a grief ritual properly may be the single most important reason for the failure of Boston's memorial games to be more than palliative.

RITUAL AND RECONCILIATION
BETWEEN YOUNG BLACK MEN

The blessing Chris received in the process of grieving his grandfather with family and friends may be partly responsible for his ability to forgive the five black boys who murdered Papa Chilli: "At the time, it made me feel good when I heard they went away for life," he stated. "But now that I'm older, when I think of all the things I've seen in my life? No, I don't want it. I don't want it. . . . These guys were 14 and 15 years old [at the time], with a lot of life ahead of them. I wish I could talk to them and tell them, 'I forgive you. Honestly.' I hate to know that they're going to be in jail for such a long time. I hate it."[16] Howard Thurman, the great mystic and theologian of the civil rights movement, once noted that a person who feels a sense of inner peace wants to see it manifest in others and in the world.[17] Chris's willingness to see the ultimate worth of those five black men certainly indicates something about the state of his inner life. At the beginning of this book I referred to the asphalt court as a representation of the objectified black male body, but Chris's memorial game for Papa Chilli (and subsequent forgiveness of those responsible for his death) turned the court into a model for the reclamation of black humanity, healing, and reconciliation.

Finally, in almost every narrative I have used to examine street basketball as a lived religion among young black men, women have been a catalyst for change and healing on the court. When young black men were able to cry, women often paved the way for their tears, supporting them, encouraging them to acknowledge their true selves. If black men are able use the basketball court in the streets and in prisons to surrender to the waters of grief inside of them, they may ultimately find that it is a tribute to the feminine energy that is the source of their lives. Chris's aunt opened the path for her nephew to grieve for Papa Chilli, and although Chris may never be able to release those five black boys from prison, his gift of forgiveness may have given them permission to free themselves.

6

THE DUNK AND THE
SIGNIFYING MONKEY

When it's played the way it's supposed to be played, basketball happens in the air, flying, floating, elevated above the floor, levitating, the way oppressed peoples of this earth imagine themselves in their dreams.

—Kareem Abdul-Jabbar, *On the Shoulders of Giants*

The 2014 Community Awareness Tournament was the marquee tournament of the summer and the final city game that Jason, C.J., and I played in together. It was special, not only because it was our last game but also due to its being infused with a sense of joy rather than sorrow. Although street basketball is often played within a context of ongoing violence, its practice sometimes moves beyond and challenges the permanence of that violent history. This chapter explores the ecstatic dimensions of street basketball, highlighting the dunk as a prototypical symbol. The dunk, in which black youth take flight above the asphalt, signifies what sociologist Michael Eric Dyson refers to as an "edifying deception"—"the ability to flout widely understood boundaries through mesmerization, a subversion of common perceptions of the culturally or physically possible through the creative and deceptive manipulation of appearance."[1]

C.J., Jason, and I were proud to be playing in Russell Paulding's Community Awareness Tournament with the names of Marvin Barros Jr. and C.J.'s cousin, Eric Paulding, across our backs. Coincidentally, when Eric was murdered, it was Marvin who stopped Russell from seeking revenge. "Marvin saw me walking down the street with redness in my eyes," Russell recalled. "He knew I was out for blood. He heard what happened to my cousin and went outside looking for me. That was the kind of person Marvin was. He cared!" Russell reflected on how Marvin forced him off the streets that day: "Let me talk to you for a second," Marvin said as he pulled Russell aside. "You're coming to my house." When Russell entered Marvin's apartment, he cornered him in the hallway, reached into Russell's waistband, and pulled out a concealed gun. "I'll be holding this. You're spending the rest of the day right here," Marvin commanded. "If Marvin hadn't come looking for me," Russell assured me, "somebody else would have died man, I'm telling you. I spent the whole day with Marvin."

Now over a decade later, we were playing ball for Marvin and Eric and another young man who had died, named Lundy. Jason and I drove together that afternoon to the basketball court. C.J. agreed to meet us there. Sticks, another close friend, agreed to follow us with his white girlfriend in the car. The fact that Julie was white was not of much concern, because I knew she would be safe at the court. White recruiters and police officers always came to these games. However, I did wonder how she would feel surrounded by almost a thousand black men and women in the heart of the inner city.

We parked our cars on Columbia Road, one of Roxbury's main streets. The sun baked the concrete as black and brown bodies moved up and down the sidewalk, sporting baggy jeans and colorful dresses. The court was at the end of a long alleyway, hidden from the main road, so we had to walk a good distance to reach the tournament. As we stepped out of the car, grabbed our bags and moved slowly toward the alleyway, I could feel the mixture of excitement and dread, especially coming from Sticks and Julie. Alleyways can feel like death traps in the city because there is no escape once you decide to enter. The walls of buildings on either side close in on you.

At the end of the alley was a group of young men, some sitting on a raised wall, others walking, congregating around them. Their presence marked the outer ring of the tournament. The tension in our bodies grew palpable as we approached them. As we inched closer the smell of marijuana wafted through the air. "Yo, what's up my nigga?!" one of the young man said to me as he approached, placing his face within inches of mine. "Corey? Wow! Is that you? How have you been?" I responded with a sense of relief that it was Corey—one of Boston's street-basketball legends. Everyone knew Corey had NBA talent, but drugs and bad choices ruined his chances. He spent his time smoking weed and hanging out on the outer circle. However, on this day I noticed something different about Corey. He seemed to be at peace.

Corey leaned into my body, almost embracing me. "Are you playing today, Naje?" "Yeah, I'm balling man. Are you?" I asked. "Yeah, I am doing it up for the kids man," he replied. "I'll get out there and run and shoot up a few threes, but man it's not about that, it's about being here and showing your face, providing inspiration for these younger guys, man. It's about being out here and just talking and reconnecting with people you haven't seen in a long time, and just doing whatever you can to show love in the community." Corey's words shocked me. I had known him when he was robbing stores and injecting steroids, and now to hear him articulate the meaning of street basketball as collective love broke open a tender place in my heart. "Wow, thank you Corey, for saying that man. That means a lot to me. I looked up to you growing up, and now to hear you say that, you came a long way man." "Yeah man," he agreed, "just getting older, man, and realizing that I have to be there for my son. I have a son now. Matter of fact, he is on the court now, wiping up everyone's sweat, and funny thing is, he is happy to do it, wiping up nigga's sweat. But that's the thing. He is looking up to everyone here. He is soaking all of this in. I told him, go and talk to your Uncle Russ, he'll give you a few dollars for wiping up the court."[2] I embraced Corey. "I love you man. Thank you for that message." "No doubt," Corey responded, as our group moved passed him towards the court. "But y'all better warm up well, 'cause I don't want to have to cross y'all asses up!" Corey shouted from a distance. We turned and laughed. "Sticks, that was one of the best ballplayers ever to grace these Boston courts man." "Wow, really?" Sticks said with excitement. Corey's smile and body language had put us at ease. We had come with the weight of the world on our shoulders. Now our burden had begun to resolve into the strangest and most wonderful sense of anticipation as we walked toward the middle ring of the court.

The beat from the speakers blared in the distance. Ice cream and food trucks, cars, and banners with the names of the dead hung against the walls. People congregated, friends greeted those who had been apart for days, weeks, even years. In front of the banner with her son's name across it was Marvin's mother. "Onaje," she said, staring at me as if she could see her son in my eyes. "Come here, let me hug you!" she said as she squeezed my body. "Mom," I said, "how have you been? I have missed you. I'm so sorry I haven't been around or called. I did see your daughters. I have been working and . . ." "Don't worry about that, Onaje. You look so good. Ah, look at you. I'm so proud of you. How is your wife?" she asked. "She is good," I responded. "My family is doing well. How is little Marvin?" When she looked at me strangely, I realized my mistake. I had meant to ask about Marvin's son, Daeshawn. "Onaje, you always calling him 'little Marvin.' You crazy boy! Your godson is doing well. He should be here later today. You know he always has to be here for his father's tournament." "I hope to see Daeshawn, Mom, I really do," I said, thankful that she had not been offended. "Well, you play well," she said. "And when I see your godson I'll send him over to you." "Okay, thanks Mom. I love you." "I love you too, boy."

It felt good to reconnect with my best friend's mom. I had always felt guilty for escaping Roxbury to an elite private school the same year he died. Why hadn't I returned to Roxbury to find his mother and the son he left behind? Was I a coward for leaving the ghetto, abandoning the people who had raised me? Marvin's mother's embrace assuaged the guilt I didn't know I had. I was still her child, her son's best friend, and she still loved me, regardless of my limitations. Her expression of love—as brief as it was—helped me accept a part of myself I had killed long ago in order to survive in mainstream culture. This Community Awareness Tournament could help mend those wounds.

I looked up at Jason who mirrored my sense of joy as he walked toward the court with a beautiful smile on his face. He had come a long way since the day we met four years ago, when he was homeless and crying because his own mother seemed to choose drugs before him. "Onaje, you, by seeing you come from the same neighborhood I did and end up teaching and studying at BU, you confirmed my struggle. I knew I had a calling from God inside me, but seeing you let me know it was real," he had explained to me.

Jason had also become more aware of his connections to ancestor spirits in the days leading up to the Community Awareness Tournament. "Onaje, I want to tell you something, I haven't told no one. You remember Dora, the lady of God?" "Yeah, I remember Dora," I nodded. "Well, the other day I was over her house and we were in her room sitting on the floor and she got real quiet. I looked over and then she got this look over her face, a strange look. Then the air in the room changed. It stood still. Everything got real strange and quiet. It's hard to explain, but it was like the air stopped moving, and I looked over at Dora and it wasn't her anymore if you know what I mean? It was her but it wasn't. And a voice came out of Dora that wasn't Dora's voice. A woman spoke from Dora's mouth. The voice said, 'Jason, this is Jessie. I have been watching you. Can you hear me?' 'Yes,' I told her I could hear her, and she was like, 'you're

meant to do great things. You are meant to be a minister of God.'
I just sat there like, yo, what is going on right now? I just sat there
and listened, and then Jessie stopped speaking and Dora came back
and started acting normal again. I was like, 'Dora, what just happened?' And Dora told me that I needed to speak to Jessie and that
she wouldn't have showed me Jessie if I wasn't ready to speak to her
like that. I have never told no one this but you, Onaje, but I just
feel like I needed to tell you. I couldn't tell just anyone. They would
think I'm crazy. Have you ever seen something like that?" I nodded my head in assurance. "When I visited Nigeria, there was one
time, I won't go into it now, but I know what you're talking about," I
responded. "Yeah, I figured you had," Jason said. "I knew you would
understand." "Listen, man," I said. "I always knew you had a gift and
I'm just thankful to know you and I can't wait to see what you do
with your gift, man. And I especially admire the way you have been
caring for your mother now, even though she still struggles with
drugs. I don't know where you get the strength, man, but I admire
you helping her fight those issues in her life."

We had come a long way together as we reached the doorway to
the inner sanctuary of the tournament. I could feel the intensity rise
in the air. Close to a thousand people were in and around the court.
"Yo, what's up Onaje? You ballin' today?" one brother asked at the
gateway. "Yeah, I'm going to be out there today," I responded with
butterflies in my stomach. "Onaje was one of the best ballplayers in
Boston," he said as he turned to an older guy leaning against a metal
railing next to the court. "You don't have to tell me that. Look at
him. His aura precedes him," the old man responded with a smile.

To make it to the inner court, we had to push through standing rows of people, positioning themselves around sidelines, spilling onto the basketball floor. The scene of so many bodies rubbing
together staring at the court was overwhelming. The smell of sweat
hung in the air; an intense beat vibrating from speakers around the
court passed through our bodies, shaking our innards. My flesh

suddenly became engulfed in an ocean of smell and sound and vibration that made it feel impossible to think. As we walked toward the bench, my head kept nodding to the beat. I noticed one player dancing on the court. He took a few dribbles, let the ball bounce on its own, gyrated his torso, waist, then lower legs. When he was done, the ball fell back into his right hand as if it had been waiting for him to finish. It was magical. No one could escape the medicine of the music as it operated on us from the inside out. I felt a deep primal connection to everyone around me, all bouncing to the same rhythm. This was belonging. This was community. This was home. This swirl of smell and sound and vibration forced me to abandon myself in the moment.

Sticks, Jason, and I made our way to the warm-up bench. C.J. had just arrived. We put our bags down and stepped onto the court in full uniform. The crowd began to whisper: "Who are these guys? What team is this?" The Community Awareness Tournament was the biggest basketball stage in the city, and we were a surprise entry. It didn't matter. Our bodies were on fire from the music, and we shot warm-up baskets like the best players in the world. Where was the energy coming from? I didn't know. Was it the crowd? The beat? Corey's embrace? Marvin's mother? Carrying Marvin, Eric, and Lundy on our backs and in our hearts? The ball? The beat? The beat.

The next forty minutes were a blur. Sticks, a six-foot-six-inch-tall forward, stepped to half-court to perform the jump ball against a six-foot-ten giant. When the ball accidentally tipped in my direction, a wiry, strong, dark-skinned kid with long braided hair and I began wrestling for it. We were so close to each other that I could feel his thoughts. Something inside me responded. Once the ball cooperated with me, I raced down the court toward the basket, eyes on the rim. A defender stood before me at the free-throw line, crouched in a defensive stance. I stopped abruptly at the three-point line. The jump shot felt lovely leaving my hands. As the ball floated across the sky, I bent my wrist and extended my fingers toward the goal. Clang! The shot ricocheted hard off the back of the rim—too much adrenaline.

The opposing team's center jumped above the rim, snatched the rebound out of the sky, and made a quick outlet for a lay-up. We were down by two. We missed our next three shots. Three minutes into the game the score was eight to zero. "Y'all gonna get blown out! Y'all better start playing some ball," one old guy yelled from the sidelines. The pressure was mounting. The same wiry guard harassed me every time I got the ball. I started sweating profusely. Dribbling up the court, I altered my rhythm so he couldn't time the movement of the ball. I glanced over at Jason. His made it clear with his eyes. He was not going to get blown out in front of this crowd. I whipped a cross-court pass toward his chest. He snatched it out of the air, faced his opponent and blew past him. He penetrated toward the left side of the basket, hung in the air, and scooped the ball off the glass. Swish! We finally had two points on the board. Next time down the court Jason took over as point guard, dribbling to the left again, this time draining a midrange jump shot. On the following play, he scored an acrobatic layup from the left baseline. We were back in the game. Now the old man responded encouragingly: "Okay, I guess y'all do got some game!"

By halftime we were in striking distance and had earned the crowd's admiration. Although the other team's point guard had been killing us with crossover moves, crisp passes, and his lightning speed, we managed to create some highlights of our own, including a tip-in layup that I snuck through the basket over their huge center. Right before we stepped back onto the court, C.J. pulled me aside: "Onaje, yo, everyone is talking about us in the crowd, especially you. Didn't you see how silent everyone got when we first stepped onto the court? They're like, yo, Onaje Woodbine's out there! They want to see if you can bring your game here at the best tournament. They're talking in the crowd." I looked at C.J. and understood that he was challenging me. He had decided to coach from our bench for most of the game and wanted to see me put on a Yale performance.

After halftime, the same wiry guard stood in front of me, this time at the top of the key. He moved his chest close to mine as I dribbled the ball in my right hand. His chin touched my collarbone. I crouched low to the ground and fed the ball between my legs from right to left. I could feel him trying to read my body language. He inched closer, crowding my legs with his torso. I found a crevice in our warm embrace and gently fed the ball between my legs from left to right. In contrast to his hard exterior, the ball passed through us like a gentle breeze. He inched closer, but I suddenly felt fear and panic run through his body. He had overcommitted. He was now at the mercy of my handle as I weaved the ball through the small openings between us in a rhythmic fashion. He thrashed his arms and flailed his body because he knew that I was about to embarrass him. In desperation, he viciously hacked down on my forearms to force the referee to stop the game. When the referee called the foul, Jason ran over to me: "Yeah, yeah, that's what I'm talking about!" I looked over at C.J. and smiled.

Unfortunately, when the other team received the ball, they were determined to beat us. All I remember next is that Sticks, Jason, and another teammate ended up hanging off of their center's shoulders as he soared above the rim. The other team's point guard made a spin move, then a crossover, jump-stopped into the lane, and darted a pinpoint chest pass into the hands of their big man. Their center launched off the floor above the paint, his two hands towering over his body with the ball, my three teammates holding onto his shoulders. Finally on his descent from the sky, he rammed the ball through the rim with such force that the entire backboard shook and swayed back and forth. Those of us below him ducked for cover. The crowd erupted into a frenzied state. Little boys were running around the court, grown men were screaming in the stands, women had their hands on their mouths. One onlooker standing under the basket starting yelling: "Who was it? Who got dunked on? Raise your hand if it was you?" He pointed to our players: "Yes, it was you, you, and you. Don't deny it!"

Strangely, however, the dunk made me smile. I looked over at Sticks, and he was also trying to hold back a grin from his face. We had just witnessed a human helicopter take flight. Marvin and Eric would have been proud. When their center came down from the sky, he was surrounded by his teammates in celebration. With this dunk his team for all intents and purposes had already won the game. In street basketball, the team that provides the most edifying experience for the crowd is the real victor. Points matter less than style. And a dunk on three people is as edifying as it gets. When the clock ran out, we grabbed our bags and went to the first row of stands on the sidelines. There was no way we were leaving this sacred space.

"Let's get this action started!" yelled a tall, dark-skinned man wearing skinny jeans with a microphone as he walked onto the court. It was the master of ceremonies. The MC's appearance was comical and strangely out of place. He paced constantly between the audience and the court as the next game started, sometimes walking directly onto the floor as if he were the eleventh player. "I heard about you. They said you got skills!" he goaded a bulky five-foot-three point guard as he stood directly behind him on the court. "But you ain't shown us nothing yet!" In response, the crafty point guard took the ball to the right corner of the basket against his defender, executed one dribble forward then a smooth step-back jump shot. The ball drilled its way through the bottom of the net. "He said not only do I shoot, but I can go to the hoop!" the MC replied, using his verbal trickery to raise the intensity of the competition. "He's got his shirt tucked in like a general!" the MC joked, describing the speedy point guard's uniform. The crowd laughed. In the loose and stylish world of street basketball it was rare to see a player wearing a uniform with military precision. But the joke was also praise. You had to respect a ballplayer who took his game that seriously. The

MC looked at the entrance to the court: "Yo, is that RJ? Shout out to RJ, coach extraordinaire of the Running Rebels and mentor to many." MCs were like this at games. One minute they were using language to create discomfort; the next they were making everyone feel at home.

"The energy in here is crazy," Jason remarked as he sat next to me on the sidelines. Two older guys behind us were schooling Jason. "You see the green team? They ain't never going to figure out the black and gold team. Ain't never! They are too unorganized, too unfocused. It might take the whole game before they figure them out." Jason laughed and nodded his head. "Yeah, you're right." I was too busy bobbing my head and moving my shoulders to the rap beats to get involved in the conversation. "Yo, what is happening to us, Onaje? This is crazy," asked Jason. "It's the beat, it's gotta be the music," I responded. "It's opening up something in us."

A lanky six-foot-nine player on the green team began prancing toward us with the basketball. He took several long strides into the paint about five feet in front of the rim. With his outstretched right arm holding the ball he took one step and leapt off the floor, ignoring the defender in front of him. At first, I couldn't wrap my mind around his intentions. He was far away from the basket so I assumed that he would shoot a one-handed floater. Instead he just kept floating upward, higher, now at least one foot above the defender in front of him. At the peak of his ascent, a gasp swept through the crowd. I felt a sudden pause in time as if the whole court was caught inside an infinite moment. His outstretched arm was the only thing that seemed to continue to move on the court. His face was so calm and tranquil as he stood there in the air. Finally this moment, which was "out of joint" from ordinary time, returned to reality. Fear washed over his face. He had become aware of being suspended in midair. Suddenly, he let go of the ball, looked downward, and stumbled back toward the floor. "Oh, my God!" Jason and I yelled with the crowd. It was the greatest play of the tournament, and he had not even touched the rim. "What just happened?" asked Jason. "Yo, I don't know," I responded. He had seemed to levitate and soar beyond what was possible. Our imaginations had flown with him.

FLYING, OTHERNESS, AND THE JOY OF HOOPS

Just "like the blues that does not make you sad," street ball can transmute grief into ecstasy. Having explored the ways grieving the dead is ritualized in hoops in the previous chapter, here I analyze one of the game's most profound celebratory moments—the dunk.[3]

If you drive through an urban area populated largely by poor and working-class black people, you may suddenly notice hundreds of residents surrounding a chain-link-fenced blacktop. Some people are sitting on the fence. Others are hanging off it to catch a glimpse of the action inside. It is loud. Anticipatory tension fills the air. If you decide to park your car, walk over toward the crowd, lean up against the fence, and peer inside to the court, you may see a familiar celebration begin to unfold.

A young man dances across the asphalt basketball court under penetrating sun. It seems like the whole city is watching him play. You notice grandmothers sitting in lawn chairs, swaying fans over their noses. Gang members pose on metal bleachers in colors representing their hood. Young women dressed in fine clothes sway hips, stare, and laugh at boys. Old men have their corner of the park as well, telling exaggerated stories of bygone basketball days. Oh, and commuters, many of them white, show up as police officers, referees, and scouts who have come to evaluate young talent for colleges, professional teams, and businesses.

As you look, you begin to focus on the young man at the center of this drama. He wears shorts and sneakers, his bare black chest aching with muscle. For a moment, he scans his surroundings, but now he goes into a defensive stance, crouching on the court, as an opposing player dribbles the ball toward him. His eyes dart in every direction. He sees the ball coming, looks over his left shoulder at the crowd, and peers to his right to find a teammate who has his back. In one fluid, sweat-dripped display of aggression and grace, he strides two long steps toward the ball, and effortlessly snatches it out of his opponent's hands. The crowd is frenzied now as he strides toward the basket with his opponent on his heels. Desperate not to be caught from behind and five feet from the hoop, he surprises everyone and launches off the pavement into the air, eyes suddenly looking down at the rim. His arms stretch out like a giraffe's neck with a basketball for a head. He rattles the rim emphatically as the ball flushes through the net and bounces hard off the forehead of his opponent who has just landed underneath him.

As this "bird in flight" comes down from the sky, he begins to celebrate.[4] Standing upright on the pavement, he spreads open his legs and arms and stomps. He tilts his head back so his pecs protrude toward the crowd. His bare knuckles pound his black-skinned chest, he screams toward the audience, his eyes bulge, and his mouth gapes open. One of his teammates approaches him, emphatically pointing to his chest and screaming as the crowd spills onto the basketball court to dance with him in frenzy.

So goes the celebration that is street basketball.

An Analysis of the Dunk: A Signified Monkey?

Notice first that the movement of this young man's body signifies both a symbiotic *and* an oppositional relationship with his neighborhood and environment, thus embodying the street-basketball world.[5]

In one sense, his bodily movements conform to normative expectations of the sports industries' and the street's image of black masculinity. In other words, his celebration is designed to acquire more capital in the eyes of his audience. He does not consciously think of it this way because his celebration is so routine, but it is possible to read his actions as a marketing strategy. Beating his protruding black chest while screaming toward the crowd bares striking resemblance to the image of a gorilla—an iconic and marketable symbol of black manhood in America. (See LeBron James, for example, on the April 2008 cover of *Vogue* magazine, holding a basketball while posing like King Kong with the petite white actress Gisele Bundchen in his grasp.)[6]

It is as if through what Pierre Bourdieu referred to as "learned ignorance" that this man senses (has "a feel for the game") that a ferocious display of his aching muscle and black skin are the perfect "raw materials" to sell, not only to outsiders and scouts but also to other black onlookers in the streets.[7] In this context, black skin is a form of cultural capital, a signal of respect and power in the street-basketball world. Pounding his chest and screaming can also be read as gestures of sexual prowess (bodily capital), reinforcing the stereotype that black men have an extraordinary desire to ravage the bodies of women. Other black male players and audience members (particularly gang members) are also impressed, particularly by the skill and exaggerated muscle flex through which he gains an edge over them (bodily capital). Even as he reenacts a limiting representation of blacks as subhuman gorillas (symbolic violence), on the asphalt this image projects power.[8]

A Signifying Monkey?

Yet this celebration is not simply a reflection of a racist, capitalist, and patriarchal culture. It is also an ironic reversal and radical critique of the dominant culture's representation of his body as monkeylike. The act of intensely pounding and pointing to his bare chest also signifies the internal presence of what some of Boston's black street-ball players refer to as "heart"—that which is innermost, deep, and the vital ground of all of life. In "The Inner Life IV: The Flow Between the Inner and the Outer," Howard Thurman addressed the religious significance of the heart in the black community and beyond. He wrote that the "heart" is a sign of the inward presence in each human being of "a resource that is as wide as life and as profound as the plunging spirit of man." This resource is the "nerve center of consent which is in each one of us" and allows us to resist all forms of dehumanization. It is the seat of a kind of embodied knowing that enters the "very ground of vitality . . . that transcends ALL of the spoken words that I can never understand through formal, discursive processes of mind."[9] Indeed, for this street-ball player, striking his chest also discloses contact with an "unnamed Something" ("an-Other") in his body, something that cannot be fully shared with words.[10] When this young man pounds his heart forcefully in celebration, he is also communicating to his audience: "I am not who you think I am! You will never know the depth of my humanity! No matter how much you try, I cannot be defined!"

By pointing to his heart concealed in his skin, he thus performs an ironic signification on his audience, cleverly turning the presumptive representation of himself as monkeylike into a radical critique of the black simian.[11] Frankly, he makes fun of his audience in secret. According to Henry Louis Gates Jr., the art of signifying is a black cultural strategy that shares similarities with the activities of trickster gods in Yoruba religious mythology in Africa and in other black religions in the Americas. To read black cultural practices as if they were "some preordained reality or thing . . . is to be duped by figuration."[12]

But acts of signification are not only designed to trick observers whose folly it is to interpret metaphorical presentations literally.[13] Signifying is also an act of mediation that brings the community into the presence of a "more."[14] By performing as tricksters, street-ball players become embodiments of the sacred who transport the community to another place.[15] As Jason remarked to me when the lanky ballplayer levitated above the paint, "What just happened?" Our imaginations had been transported beyond the confines of the ghetto. Through radical movements and style, these ballplayers communicate this "unnamed Something" and push the community of onlookers to abandon presupposing activities.[16] As mediators within the black ritual ground of the court, street-basketball players serve powerful ritual purposes.[17] They embody the heart that serves the community by generating joy and hope among the audience.

The pastoral psychologist Gregory C. Ellison II defines hope "as a desire for existential change generated and sustained in a community of reliable others that names difficulties, envisions new possibilities and inspires work toward transformation of self and other."[18] During the Community Awareness Tournament the three rings of the court formed a communal container of "reliable others," and these caregivers provoked a desire for existential change in Jason and me. Ellison suggests that individuals who possess the ability to feel hope often internalize it through the experience of being cared for by others. Particularly in infancy, a child will internalize the reliability of its parental figures as a basis for developing hopefulness as a basic quality of character. The developmental psychologist Erik Erikson contended that a hopeful personality is actually won or lost in infancy. But Ellison disagrees sharply with Erikson, suggesting that a "hopeful self" can be formed outside of the immediate family and into adulthood.

This "generativist" view of hope is critical for Ellison because he serves "a population of African American young men who are substantially at risk of being muted and made invisible. This muteness and invisibility threatens hope and results from numerous factors[:] . . . fewer opportunities for higher educations . . . incarceration . . . dehumanizing portrayals in history and the modern media. . . . Lacking positive recognition and affirmation early in life, the development of a hopeful self may prove challenging."[19] A question worth asking then, is where and when do marginalized young black men in U.S. cities engender hope?

Celebratory practices on street-basketball courts can serve as important generators of hope among this population of invisible black men. As with the dunk celebration, street-ball-community members have the capacity to become "reliable others," sharing their "heart" and responding with recognition and joy. When teammates point to each other's chests and scream in frenzy, they function as empathic mirrors, countering muteness and invisibility among themselves. As tricksters, these ballplayers sustain human life in the absence of the material means to do so, "nam[ing] difficulties, envision[ing] new possibilities, and inspir[ing]" through the style with which they play the game.

Striking the chest, therefore, is *both* a strategy designed to obtain power and favor and a dance through which street-ball players play with the ineffable.[20] This double meaning, as an expression of what W. E. B. Du Bois called "double consciousness,"[21] illustrates the creative relationship between the "hardness of life" that black street-ball players endure within an opaque culture and the religious experience that permeates its facade. In these communities' ritualized experiences of grieving and celebrating on the court, players are attempting to become aware of their humanity in a dehumanizing situation and are struggling to assert and express the same in social life.

After we watched a couple more games during the Community Awareness Tournament, our hearts aflutter, Jason and I made our way toward the exit. C.J. had wandered off into the crowd somewhere, and Sticks and Julie had left almost immediately after our game was done. (I later discovered that Julie felt out of place, sitting in a sea of black people near the court, unceasing noise of rap beats in her ears.) Jason and I, however, were overjoyed. The music, the smells, the game, the people, and the dunk: our bodies had been unburdened. Near the exit we spotted a group of older women and young men selling sweet barbecued and fried chicken. Their shirts read "Chicken Gawds." We were in heaven. Food in hand, we exited the doorway and returned to the streets of Roxbury.

EPILOGUE

During the course of researching this book it became clear that street basketball was a way of life for many young black men in Boston. These men carried their most precious concerns to the asphalt, where they attempted to rework and reimagine the problems of inner-city life. While they sometimes invoked normative theological categories and symbols to communicate these experiences, they generally sidestepped doctrine in favor of truths experienced in blood and flesh. Their urban "lived religion," was expressed through rhythms, sounds, styles, symbols, transcendent experiences, and rituals.

At the same time, there were limitations regarding their attempts to reclaim a sense of humanity beyond the constraints of their historical situation. In particular, their grieving practices, while palliative, rarely led to a sense of wholeness or healing. The primary reason for this failure was the absence of a critical mass of elders to bestow a sense of blessing and recognition before, during, and after these games. With this in mind and in the interest of promoting a paradigm shift in how young black men relate to one another and to their larger environment, I ask our elders a common street-basketball refrain: who's got next? Who's got next to transform our urban basketball courts into conscious ritual space by which to change the generational trauma of embodied oppression, thereby reclaiming memory and opening our path toward wholeness? Who's got next?

WHO'S GOT NEXT?

past the chain link fence
deep in the center
there is juju
juju enough to
change
your mind
who's got next?
blankets the court
and
hope rests embodied in
the question the
crucible
of the asphalt begs
who's got next?
beyond the mundane chains
there is magic
magic enough to
change
your heart
there we are ushered
through
the pains by Spirits
Known and
Unknown their dark
matter bending space
infused into
the blacktops
are our
mothers' wombs
blending time
laboring

with dark energies
invoked by the libation of
our tears
and
the altar of our bodies
wanting love
we sweat profusely
praying this time
the dance
of our black bodies
on the asphalt
brings
the relief
so needed
and
past the
crossover can
we
cross over
to embrace one
and others and
know
we are still
men in need of love?
who's got next?
on the other side of the fence
there is Nommo
Nommo enough to change
your spirit there
to Know
our manhood cannot
be earned shedding one
and others' blood,

but is nestled
inside the soft
and
powerful
gifts of
forgiveness
and
respect
who's got next?
an ancestral refrain
with presumed inclusion
to dis play your
Self on the altar
of the blacktop
naked and unashamed
this sacred space
refines your mettle
is safe harbor with
waters of the wombs
to wash us anew
and
in the night
long after we
are absent from
the court
it gestates and
waits to embrace
who's got next

Robert J. Woodbine

My father and friend, Dr. Robert J. Woodbine, earned his doctor-
ate in naturopathic medicine and his masters in acupuncture and

oriental medicine. He is the executive director of Urban Qi Foundation, Inc. He wrote this poem after many conversations with me regarding the intergenerational impact of institutional racism on black men and their children.

NOTES

INTRODUCTION

1. Onaje Woodbine, "Why I'm Quitting Basketball," *Yale Alumni Magazine*, November 2000.
2. Jacques Derrida, *Specters of Marx: The State of the Debt, the Work of Mourning, and the New International*, trans. Peggy Kamuf (New York: Routledge, 1994), 54.
3. Clifford Geertz, "Deep Play: Notes on the Balinese Cockfight," *Myth, Symbol and Culture* 101, no. 1 (Winter 1972): 83.
4. Hershini Young, *Haunting Capital: Memory, Text, and the Black Diasporic Body* (Hanover, NH: Dartmouth University Press, 2005), 8.
5. This section is greatly indebted to Nancy Ammerman, "Lived Religion," in *Emerging Trends in the Social and Behavioral Sciences: An Interdisciplinary, Searchable, and Linkable Resource* (Hoboken, NJ: Wiley Online Library, 2015), 1–8, http://onlinelibrary.wiley.com/doi/10.1002/9781118900772.etrds0207 /abstract.
6. Charles H. Long, *Significations: Signs, Symbols, and Images in the Interpretation of Religion* (Philadelphia: Fortress Press, 1986), 7.
7. See Pierre Bourdieu and Loïc Wacquant, *An Invitation to Reflexive Sociology* (Chicago: University of Chicago Press, 1992). For this understanding of Bourdieu's sociology of practice, I am greatly indebted to my mentor and friend, the religious studies scholar Christopher R. Lehrich.
8. "In these exceptional moments of crisis, of time 'out of joint,' ghosts signal our inheritance of the past and the necessity to act responsibly to change the future" (Young, *Haunting*, 41).
9. John Hoberman, *Darwin's Athletes: How Sport Has Damaged Black America and Preserved the Myth of Race* (Boston: Mariner Books, 1997).

10. Scott N. Brooks, "Just a Dream? Structure, Power, and Agency in Basketball," in *Sport and Challenges to Racism*, ed. Jonathan Long and Karl Spracklen (Houndmills, Basingstoke: Palgrave Macmillan, 2010), 144.

11. I have borrowed this method of analysis and phrasing from Pierre Bourdieu and Loïc Wacquant. Wacquant discusses Bourdieu's objections to structural analyses of social behavior that, paradoxically, overlook the practices they seek to explain: "The chief danger of the objectivist point of view is that, lacking a principle of generation of those regularities, it tends to slip from model to reality—to reify the structures it constructs by treating them as autonomous entities endowed with the ability to 'act' in the manner of historical agents. Incapable of grasping practice other than negatively, as the mere *execution* of the model built by the analyst, objectivism ends up projecting into the minds of agents a (scholastic) vision of their practice that, paradoxically, it could only uncover because it methodically set aside the experience agents have of it" (Bourdieu and Wacquant, *Invitation*, 8).

12. Young, *Haunting*, 31.

13. On being "known," see Scott Brooks, "City of Basketball Love: Philadelphia and the Nurturing of Black Male Hoop Dreams," *Journal of African American History* 96, no. 4 (Fall 2011): 522–536. Also see Scott Brooks, *Black Men Can't Shoot* (Chicago: University of Chicago Press, 2009). Brooks's ethnography of street basketball in Philadelphia is a masterful depiction of how poor, young, black men work hard to become "known" and achieve status as basketball players.

14. See Pierre Bourdieu et al., *The Weight of the World: Social Suffering in Contemporary Society*, trans. Priscilla Parkhurst Ferguson (Stanford, Calif.: Stanford University Press, 1999), for a discussion of the value of "social proximity" between researchers and subjects.

15. Bourdieu defines symbolic violence as "violence which is wielded precisely inasmuch as one does not perceive it as such.... Being born in a social world, we accept a whole range of postulates, axioms, which go without saying and require no inculcating. This is why the analysis of the doxic acceptance of the world, due to the immediate agreement of objective structures and cognitive structures, is the true foundation of a realistic theory of domination and politics. Of all forms of 'hidden persuasion,' the most implacable is the one exerted, quite simply, by the *order of things*" (Bourdieu and Wacquant, *Invitation*, 168).

16. This "something more" is a reference to William James's definition of religious consciousness: "It is as if there were in the human consciousness a sense of reality, a feeling of objective presence, a perception of what we may call 'something there,' more deep and more general than any of the special and particular 'senses' by which the current psychology supposes existent realities

to be originally revealed" (*The Varieties of Religious Experience: A Study in Human Nature* [1902; New York: Random House, 1999], 58).

17. "Like the blues that does not make you sad even though it is about that emotion, black preaching, while having its point of departure in the depths of the moan's historicity, moves beyond that to a joyful and courageous affirmation of being. The shout is the opaque utterance expressing what more trained black clergy were saying in standard English" (James Noel, *Black Religion and the Imagination of Matter in the Atlantic World* [New York: Palgrave Macmillan, 2009], 153).

18. Gregory Ellison II, *Cut Dead but Still Alive: Caring for African American Young Men* (Nashville, Tenn.: Abingdon Press, 2013).

1. "LAST ONES LEFT" IN THE GAME: FROM BLACK RESISTANCE TO URBAN EXILE

1. Martin Finucane, "City Residents Reeling after Mattapan Slayings," *Boston Globe*, September 28, 2010, http://www.boston.com/news/local/breaking _news/2010/09/five_shot_three.html. In addition, see Walter Fluker, "Cultural Asylums and the Jungles Planted in Them: The Exilic Condition of African American Males and the Black Church," presented at Religious Practices in Global Contexts: "Religion, Conflict, and Peacemaking," Boston University School of Theology, Spring 2011, available at http://www.bu.edu /sth/files/2013/06/Fluker-Cultural-Asylums.pdf.

2. The Urban League of Eastern Massachusetts attempted to offer a positive spin on Boston's racial inequities, noting "amity" between racial and ethnic groups had increased. Their report also noted an increase in the number of black politicians and black-owned businesses. However, these gains for a small minority of black professionals were far outweighed by the huge racial disparities in health, criminal justice, and poverty for the majority of Boston's black residents. Tulaine S. Marshall and Jacqui Conrad, eds., "State of Black Boston 2011: Good News and Good Work to Be Done" (Urban League of Eastern Massachusetts, 2011), available at https://docs.google.com /file/d/0Bx93m3UUyugcbHV5VkN2YkdwLUE/edit?pli=1.

3. My understanding of the terms "structural violence" and "racial injury" is informed by Hussein Bulhan's definition: "Structural violence is a feature of social structures. This form of violence is inherent in the established modes of social relations, distribution of goods and services, and legal practices of dispensing justice. . . . Structural violence in particular imposes a pattern of relations and practices that are deeply ingrained in and dominate everyday living. . . . Structural violence enjoys sanctions of ruling authorities and

appears diffuse and very much linked with *social reality*" (*Frantz Fanon and the Psychology of Oppression* [New York: Plenum Press, 1985], 136).

4. Marshall and Conrad, "State of Black Boston 2011."

5. Ibid.

6. Netherworlds or underworlds are places where departed souls venture soon after death according to many of the world's religious mythologies. Particularly in indigenous cultures, the souls of the deceased communicate with the living from these sacred places within the earth. The literary scholar Willie Perdoma reminded me that in New York City, from the perspective of high-rise government-housing-project buildings, street-basketball courts appear to be located beneath the ground.

7. Bourdieu describes *habitus* as a "living memory pad": "Enacted belief, instilled by childhood learning that treats the body as a living memory pad, an automation that leads the mind unconsciously along it and as a repository of the most precious values, is the form par excellence of the blind and symbolic thought" (*The Logic of Practice*, trans. Richard Nice [Stanford, Calif.: Stanford University Press, 1992], 62).

8. For Bourdieu's description of a "sense of the game," see Pierre Bourdieu and Loïc Wacquant, *An Invitation to Reflexive Sociology* (Chicago: University of Chicago Press, 1992), 120–121.

9. Michael Eric Dyson suggests that improvisation is an important mode of expression in African American culture, particularly in black basketball. Referring to improvisation as the "will to spontaneity," Dyson defines it is as "the way in which historical accidence is transformed into cultural advantage, and the way acts of apparently random occurrence are spontaneously and imaginatively employed by Africans and African Americans in a variety of forms of cultural expression" ("Be Like Mike? Michael Jordan and the Pedagogy of Desire," in *Between Borders: Pedagogy and the Politics of Cultural Studies*, ed. Henry A. Giroux and Peter McLaren [New York: Routledge, 1994], 121).

10. William C. Rhoden, *Forty Million Dollar Slaves: The Rise, Fall, and Redemption of the Black Athlete* (New York: Three Rivers Press, 2006), 171.

11. Here I am thinking of Ludwig Wittgenstein's aphorism: "what can be shown, cannot be said" (*Tractatus Logico-Philosophicus*, trans. D. F. Pears and B. F. McGuiness [London: Routledge and Kegan Paul, 1963], 51. Charles H. Long suggests that Wittgenstein's aphorism means "what shows itself is prior to speech and language and the basis for speech and language; furthermore, because it shows itself, it cannot be said—it is silent" (Long, *Significations: Signs, Symbols, and Images in the Interpretation of Religion* [Philadelphia: Fortress Press, 1986], 60–61).

12. For an excellent study of the "exilic condition" of urban black males, see Fluker, "Cultural Asylums and the Jungles Planted in Them."

13. James Naismith, *Basketball: Its Origin and Development* (Lincoln: University of Nebraska Press, 1996), 23.

14. William J. Baker, introduction to Naismith, *Basketball*, xi, xii.

15. Nina Mjagkij, *Light in the Darkness: African Americans and the YMCA, 1852–1946* (Lexington: University Press of Kentucky, 2003), 1.

16. Clifford Putney, *Muscular Christianity: Manhood and Sports in Protestant America, 1880–1920* (Cambridge, Mass.: Harvard University Press, 2001), 8.

17. Mjagkij, *Light*, 1.

18. This section is greatly indebted to historian Claude Johnson, *Black Fives: The Alpha Physical Culture Club's Pioneering African American Basketball Team, 1904–1923* (Greenwich, CT: Black Fives Publishing, 2012), Kindle edition, chapter 1.

19. Ibid.

20. Ibid., chapter 2.

21. Ibid.

22. Ibid.

23. Gena Caponi-Tabery suggests that there was a confluence of sports, music, and dance in black culture during the 1930s. In particular, she argues that the "jump" became a symbolic gesture of transcendence and joy among blacks in basketball, blues music and Lindy Hop dance across the country: "Jump tunes, the jumping jitterbug, and jump shots all burst out of the same arenas, at a time when dance bands traveled with basketball teams and clubs across the country hosted predance basketball games. These forms of expressive culture are connected through site, impulse, cultural meaning, and common gesture. . . . Reflecting 'the accelerated tempo of black life during and after the urban migration as well as an upbeat sense of expanded possibility,' nothing better captured the feeling of spiritual uplift and hopes for upward mobility than this intersection of dance, music and sport. The jump symbolized and expressed joy in the present and optimism for the future" ("Jump for Joy: Jump Blues, Dance, and Basketball in 1930s African America," in *Sports Matters: Race, Recreation, and Culture*, ed. John Bloom and Michael Nevin Willard [New York: New York University Press, 2002], 39–40.

24. *On the Shoulders of Giants*, directed by Deborah Morales (S.I.: Union Productions, 2011), DVD.

25. For an excellent study of the role of the Harlem Globetrotters in the integration of American basketball and as a precursor to white exploitation of black athletes in hoops, see Ben Green, *Spinning the Globe: The Rise, Fall, and Return to Greatness of the Harlem Globetrotters* (New York: Amistad, 2006).

26. Bobbito Garcia, foreword to Johnson, *Black Fives*.

27. *On the Shoulders of Giants*.

28. Jealous expressed these thoughts after the acquittal of Trayvon Martin's killer:

Our generation of black Americans was supposed to be the first not to be judged by our race or the color of our skin. Instead, we had come of age to find ourselves the most incarcerated on the planet and most murdered in the country.

"Grandma," I would ask days later, still searching for understanding: "What happened? How did things turn out like this?"

Her response was the crux of my speech to the 104th NAACP convention yesterday. She leaned in and spoke softly: "It's sad but it's simple: We got what we fought for, but we lost what we had."

Benjamin Jealous, "Zimmerman Verdict: Keep Fighting," *Skanner*, July 16, 2013, http://www.theskanner.com/opinion/commentary/19207/zimmerman -verdict-keep-fighting-2013-07-16.

29. William Julius Wilson, *The Truly Disadvantaged: The Inner City, the Underclass, and Public Policy* (Chicago: University of Chicago Press, 1987), 58.

30. William Oliver suggests that "for many marginalized Black males, 'the streets' is a socialization institution that is as important as the family, the church, and the educational system in terms of its influence on their psychosocial development and life course trajectories and transitions." Drawing from Elijah Anderson's ethnographic studies of black urban life, Oliver suggests that "high rates of unemployment, underemployment, poverty, substance abuse, incarceration, and inadequate family and fatherhood role functioning are major characteristics of Black males who center their lives in 'the streets'" ("'The Streets': An Alternative Black Male Socialization Institution," *Journal of Black Studies* 36, no. 6 [2006]: 919).

31. I learned this story from DJ Bobbito Garcia, whom I interviewed on January 17, 2013. Garcia was the co-host of the "The Stretch Armstrong and Bobbito Show," considered by many to be the best hip-hop radio show of all time. He is also an author, announcer, and film producer of playground basketball in New York City. His most recent project is a documentary entitled *Doin' It in the Park: Pick-Up Basketball, NYC*, directed by Bobbito Garcia and Kevin Couliau (New York: Goldcrest Films, 2012), DVD. The film documents the fact that rappers, break-dancers, and ballplayers performed together on the same playgrounds.

32. Vincent Mallozzi, *Asphalt Gods: An Oral History of Rucker Park* (New York: Doubleday, 2003), 9.

33. *Fathers of the Sport*, directed by Xavier Mitchell (Fayetteville, Ark.: Hannover House, 2013), DVD.

34. Ibid.

35. See Anthony Pinn's humanistic definition of black religion "as *the recognition of a response to the elemental feeling for complex subjectivity and the accompanying transformation of consciousness that allows for the historically manifest battle*

against the terror of fixed identity. While this experience may not result in sustained sociopolitical and cultural transformation, it does involve a new life meaning that encourages continued struggle for a more liberated existence" (*Terror and Triumph: The Nature of Black Religion* [Minneapolis, Minn.: Augsburg Fortress Publishers, 2003], 175).

2. BOSTON'S MEMORIAL GAMES

1. Pierre Bourdieu, *The Weight of the World: Social Suffering in Contemporary Society* (Stanford, Calif.: Stanford University Press, 2000), 614.

2. Ibid., 615.

3. Durkheim defined religion as "a unified system of beliefs and practices relative to sacred things, i.e., things set apart and forbidden—beliefs and practices which unite in one moral community called a Church, all those who adhere to them" (*The Elementary Forms of the Religious Life*, trans. Joseph Ward Swain [1915; New York: Free Press, 1965], 62).

4. Bourdieu's theory of social practice has been described as being capable of accounting for the elusive quality of a "bird in flight." See Annette Lareau and Erin McNamara Horvat, "Moments of Social Inclusion and Exclusion: Race, Class, and Cultural Capital in Family-School Relationships," *Sociology of Education* 72, no. 1 (January 1999): 38.

5. Brooks suggests that one of the ways to become a "known" city basketball player is to have other players "vouch" for you. When a "known" player vouches for an unknown player, he confers a modicum of status to that player. Scott N. Brooks, *Black Men Can't Shoot* (Chicago: University of Chicago Press, 2009).

6. Leagues tend to cost more money and take more time to organize than tournaments; therefore, they are often organized by established institutions such as community centers, churches, or the city.

7. For an analysis of Carrie Mae Weems's photograph of an "empty chair" in her series on the Gullah Sea Islands, see Hershini Young, *Haunting Capital: Memory, Text, and the Black Diasporic Body* (Hanover, NH: Dartmouth University Press, 2005), 3.

8. Marvin's mother, Doris Barros, explained to me that Marvin understood the symbol of the "bird" in Christian terms as a representation of the Holy Spirit.

9. James P. McFadden, "PBHA Students Grieve Killing of Local Teen," *Harvard Crimson*, December, 15, 1997.

10. Jim Jones, "Rain," *Pray IV Reign*, Columbia / Ether Boy 88697 19376, 2009, CD.

11. Sam Cooke, "A Change Is Gonna Come," *Ain't That Good News*, RCA Victor LSP-2899, 1964, LP.

12. Chuck Miller, "The 2011 Louis Saunders Memorial Basketball Tournament," Timesunion.com, August 3, 2011, http://blog.timesunion.com/chuckmiller/the-2011-louis-saunders-memorial-basketball-tournament/9656/.
13. *He Got Game*, directed by Spike Lee (Burbank, Calif.: Touchstone Pictures and Forty Acres & a Mule Filmworks, 1998), DVD.
14. Maria Cramer and Brian R. Ballou, "Playing Scared: A Neighborhood Reflects as Teen Killed on Court Is Mourned," *Boston Globe*, May 12, 2010.

3. JASON, HOOPS, AND GRANDMA'S HHANDS

1. Joseph C. Scriven, "What a Friend We Have in Jesus," in *Pilgrim Hymnal* (Boston: Pilgrim Press, 1968), 335.

4. C.J., HOOPS, AND THE QUEST
FOR A SECOND LIFE

1. Fortunately, toward the end of my studies, there were several white professors in the religion department and a few professors of color who were affiliated with the religion department who did enthusiastically support my research. For them, I am grateful.
2. Howard Thurman discussed the devastation to the self when one remains unrecognized by others: "It is a strange freedom to be adrift in the world of men without a sense of anchor anywhere. Always there is a need of mooring, the need for the firm grip on something that is rooted and will not give. The urge to be accountable to someone, to know that beyond the individual himself there is an answer that must be given, cannot be denied. The deed a man performs must be weighed in a balance held by another's hand. The very spirit of a man tends to panic from the desolation of going nameless up and down the street of other minds where no salutation greets and no friendly recognition makes secure. It is a strange freedom to be adrift in the world of men" (*The Inward Journey* [Richmond, Ind.: Friends United Press, 1971], 37–38).
3. This section of C.J.'s testimony is also reprinted in Onaje Woodbine, "An Invisible Institution: A Functional Approach to Religion in Sports in Wounded African American Communities," in *The Black Church and Hip Hop Culture: Toward Bridging the Generational Divide*, ed. Emmett G. Price III (Lanham, Md.: Scarecrow Press, 2011), 177–178.

5. ANCESTOR WORK IN STREET BASKETBALL

1. "Chris Paul Pays Tribute to His Grandfather in 2002," *ESPN Sports Center Flashback*, May 8, 2008, https://www.youtube.com/watch?v=fxwyE5m44x4.

2. Malidoma Patrice Some, *Ritual: Power, Healing, and Community* (New York: Penguin Books, 1997).
3. Arnold van Gennep, *The Rites of Passage* (Chicago: University of Chicago Press, 1961).
4. Dwayne A. Tunstall, "Taking Africana Existential Philosophy of Education Seriously," *Philosophical Studies in Education* 39 (2008): 48.
5. Ibid., 46.
6. Some, *Ritual*, 32.
7. "Reality-testing has shown that the loved object no longer exists, and it proceeds to demand that all libido shall be withdrawn from its attachments to that object. This demand arouses understandable opposition—it is a matter of general observation that people never willingly abandon a libidinal position, not even, indeed, when a substitute is already beckoning to them. This opposition can be so intense that a turning away from reality takes place and a clinging to the object through the medium of a hallucinatory wishful psychosis" (Sigmund Freud, "Mourning and Melancholia," in *The Standard Edition of the Complete Psychological Works of Sigmund Freud, Volume XIV (1914–1916): On the History of the Psycho-Analytic Movement, Papers on Metapsychology and Other Works* [New York: Norton, 1976], 243).
8. "Chris Paul Pays Tribute."
9. Éva Tettenborn, "Melancholia as Resistance in Contemporary African American Literature," *MELUS* 31, no. 3 (Fall 2006): 101–121.
10. Toni Morrison, *Beloved* (New York: Vintage, 2004), 244.
11. "Chris Paul Pays Tribute."
12. Ibid.
13. Some, *Ritual*, 76.
14. "Chris Paul Pays Tribute."
15. Ibid.
16. Ibid.
17. Howard Thurman, "Mysticism and Social Change," October 28, 1938, Howard Thurman Collection, Box 17, Howard Gotlieb Archival Research Center, Boston University.

6. THE DUNK AND THE SIGNIFYING MONKEY

1. Michael Eric Dyson, "Be Like Mike? Michael Jordan and the Pedagogy of Desire," *Cultural Studies* 7 (1993): 68.
2. Russell Paulding holds his tournament indoors to avoid injuries. However, the gym is off of Columbia Road down an alleyway and opens out on one side through several double doors so that it feels like the court is outside. In fact, the intermediate ring of onlookers stands outside, stretching, eating food, socializing, and peeking at the game.

3. James Noel, *Black Religion and the Imagination of Matter in the Atlantic World* (New York: Palgrave Macmillan, 2009), 153. There is no shortage of commentary in the media about the celebratory practices of African American men in amateur and professional sports, particularly in football and basketball. In the film *White Men Can't Jump*, for example, Billy Hoyle (Woody Harrelson) expresses the general belief that black athletes' celebrations signify egoism. After losing a major basketball game, Billy reprimands Sidney Deane (Wesley Snipes): "You're like every other brother I ever saw. You'd rather look good and lose than look bad and win" (*White Men Can't Jump*, directed by Ron Shelton [Beverly Hills, Calif.: Twentieth-Century Fox Film Corporation, 1992], DVD).

4. On the idea of the "bird in flight," see Annette Lareau and Erin McNamara Horvat, "Moments of Social Inclusion and Exclusion: Race, Class, and Cultural Capital in Family-School Relationships," *Sociology of Education* 72, no. 1 (January 1999): 38.

5. Loïc Wacquant, *Body and Soul: Notebooks of an Apprentice Boxer* (New York: Oxford University Press, 2004).

6. My understanding of the marketability of black men as dangerous monkey beasts is greatly indebted to the work of Clinton R. Fluker, "Meet King Kong," Mellon Fellowship Paper, Morehouse and Spelman Colleges, May 2008; and Walter E. Fluker, "Cultural Asylums and the Jungles Planted in Them: The Exilic Condition of African American Males and the Black Church," presented at Religious Practices in Global Contexts: "Religion, Conflict, and Peacemaking," Boston University School of Theology, Spring 2011, http://www.bu.edu/sth/files/2013/06/Fluker-Cultural-Asylums.pdf. For examples, see *Birth of a Nation*, directed by D. W. Griffith (1915; New York: Kino on Video, 2002), DVD; *King Kong*, directed by Peter Jackson (Universal City, Calif.: Universal Pictures, 2005), DVD; *Training Day*, directed by Antoine Fuqua (Burbank, Calif.: Warner Brothers, 2001), DVD; and the April 2008 *Vogue* cover with LeBron James and Gisele Bundchen at "Commentary: Photos of Black Subjects Covered with Controversy," *Pittsburgh Post-Gazette*, April 1, 2008, http://www.post-gazette.com/life/lifestyle/2008/04/01/Commentary-Photos-of-black-subjects-covered-with-controversy/stories/200804010228.

7. Bourdieu defines the concept of "learned ignorance" as follows: "In short, one has quite simply to bring into scientific work and in to the theory of practices that it seeks to produce, a theory—which cannot be found through theoretical experience alone—of what it is to be a 'native,' that is, to be in that relationship of 'learned ignorance,' of immediate but unselfconscious understanding which defines the practical relationship to the world" (*The Logic of Practice* [Stanford, Calif.: Stanford University Press, 1990], 19). See also Pierre Bourdieu and Loïc

J. D. Wacquant, *An Invitation to Reflexive Sociology* (Chicago: University of Chicago Press, 1992), 120–121.

8. "Symbolic violence," for Bourdieu is "violence which is wielded precisely inasmuch as one does not perceive it as such. . . . Being born in a social world, we accept a whole range of postulates, axioms, which go without saying and require no inculcating. This is why the analysis of the doxic acceptance of the world, due to the immediate agreement of objective structures and cognitive structures, is the true foundation of a realistic theory of domination and politics. Of all forms of 'hidden persuasion,' the most implacable is the one exerted, quite simply, by the order of things" (Bourdieu and Wacquant, *Invitation*, 168).

9. Howard Thurman, "The Inner Life IV: The Flow Between the Inner and the Outer," 1952, Howard Thurman Collection, Howard Gotlieb Archival Research Center, Boston University.

10. Charles H. Long insists that an African American has had to "experience the truth of his negativity and at the same time transform and create an-other reality. Given the limitation imposed upon him, he created on the level of his religious consciousness" (*Significations: Signs, Symbols, and Images in the Interpretation of Religion* [Aurora, Colo.: Davies Group Publishers, 1999], 177).

11. I am greatly indebted to Henry Louis Gates's theory of the discursive role of the "signifying monkey" in black folk and literary culture. Gates explains that the "signifying monkey," an African American trickster figure, is an "ironic reversal of a received racist image of the black as simianlike, the Signifying Monkey— he who dwells at the margins of discourse, ever punning, ever troping, ever embodying the ambiguities of language—is our trope for repetition and revision, indeed, is our trope of chiasmus itself, repeating and simultaneously reversing in one deft, discursive act" ("'The Blackness of Blackness': A Critique of the Sign and the Signifying Monkey," *Critical Inquiry* 9, no. 4 [1983]: 686). Bourdieu makes a similar argument, noting that the "logic of symbolic domination" necessitates that the dominated use symbols from the dominant culture to express resistance. As Wacquant puts it, "Bourdieu rejects the alternative of submission and resistance that has traditionally framed the question of dominated cultures and which, in his eyes, prevents us from adequately understanding practices and situations that are often defined by their intrinsically double, skewed nature. . . . To resist I have no means other than to make mine and to claim aloud the very properties that mark me as dominated (according to the paradigm 'black is beautiful')" (Bourdieu and Wacquant, *Invitation*, 28).

12. Gates, "Blackness of Blackness," 723. "The Signifying Monkey is a trickster figure, of the order of the trickster figure of Yoruba mythology, Esu-Elegbara in Nigeria, and Legba among the Fon in Dahomey, whose New

World figurations . . . speak eloquently of the unbroken arc of metaphysical presuppositions and patterns of figuration shared through space and time among black cultures in West Africa, South America, the Caribbean, and the United States. The trickster figures, aspects of Esu, are primarily mediators: as tricksters they are mediators and their mediations are tricks" (ibid., 687).

13. Claudia Mitchell-Kernan offers a lucid definition of signifying as a linguistic style in black culture: "The Black concept of signifying incorporates essentially a folk notion that dictionary entries for words are not always sufficient for interpreting meaning or messages, or that meaning goes beyond such interpretations. . . . A particular utterance may be an insult in one context and not another. . . . The hearer is thus constrained to attend to all potential meaning carrying symbolic systems—the total universe of discourse" ("Signifying, Loud-Talking, and Marking," in *Signifyin(g), Sanctifyin', and Slam Dunking*, ed. Gena Dagel Caponi [Amherst: University of Massachusetts Press, 1999], 311).

14. The religion scholar Joseph Murphy defines the role of tricksters in African Diaspora spiritual traditions as mediators that serve as bridges between the living community and the world of spirit. He uses the example of the trickster figure Legba, otherwise known as Elegbara or Esu in several black religious traditions, including Yoruba and Voodoo. "Legba is an old man who walks with a stick. . . . He is . . . an original trickster, with his mind in two worlds. And so he becomes a gatekeeper between the worlds. . . . When he opens the gate, the two worlds can interpenetrate" (*Working the Spirit: Ceremonies of the African Diaspora* [Boston: Beacon Press, 1994], 39).

15. Murphy suggests that African Diasporic religious rites are primarily oriented toward serving the community: "Diasporan spirituality can be recognized by its . . . reciprocity of spirit and human being, and its sharing of the spirit in the service of community" (ibid., 185).

16. Murphy frames the religions of the African Diaspora as "systems of action" rather than "systems of belief." He notes that the major "texts" of these religions are transmitted "orally and ceremonially." There is a "high interdependency between the idea of spirit and the actions which incarnate it. In a sense the spirit is the action of the community" (ibid., 182). He illustrates the interdependency of theory and practice in black preaching: "Nearly every witness of African American preaching has tried to convey that it is the style of the delivery of the sermon as much as the content which is important to the congregation. The preference for ceremonial precision over systematic thought indicates an alternative spirituality" (183). For an excellent analysis of the theme of embodiment in the religions of the African Diaspora, see chapter 6 in Stephen Prothero, *God Is Not One* (New York: HarperOne, 2010). Also see Yvonne Daniel, *Dancing Wisdom: Embodied Knowledge in Haitian Vodou,*

Cuban Yoruba, and Bahian Candomble (Urbana: University of Illinois Press, 2005).

17. Robert B. Stepto explores the social and religious functions of African American ritual space from slavery to the present. His definition and description of African American ritual grounds is worth quoting at length: African American ritual grounds are "special configurations within the structural topography that are, in varying ways, elaborate responses to social structure in this world. . . . The slave quarters are, I think, the prototypical ritual ground, not only because they constituted the first space within social structure redefined in some measure by Afro-Americans, but also because they serve as a spatial expression of the tensions and contradictions besetting any reactionary social structure, aggressive or latent, subsumed by a dominant social structure. The grand tension is that of self-initiated mobility versus self-imposed confinement: ritual grounds . . . offer the exhilarating prospect of community, protection, progress, learning, and a religious life while often birthing and even nurturing (usually unintentionally) a sense of enclosure that may reach claustrophobic proportions. In short, Afro-American ritual grounds are quite frequently, in the final analysis, spatial expressions within a structured topography of the 'double life, with double thoughts, double duties, and double social classes' giving rise to 'double words and double ideals' that characterize what Du Bois describes to be the Negro's burden of 'double consciousness'" (*From Behind the Veil: A Study of Afro-American Narrative* [Urbana: University of Illinois Press, 1991], 68–69).

18. Gregory C. Ellison II, "Late Stylin' in an Ill-Fitting Suit: Donald Capps' Artistic Approach to the Hopeful Self and Its Implications for Unacknowledged African American Young Men," *Pastoral Psychology* 58 (2009): 485.

19. Ibid., 484.

20. Wacquant explains Bourdieu's "double reading" of culture: "Social facts are objects which are also the object of knowledge within reality itself because human beings make meaningful the world which makes them. A science of society thus understood as a bidimensional 'system of relations of power and relations of meaning between groups and classes' must of necessity effect a double reading" (Bourdieu and Wacquant, *Invitation*, 7).

21. W. E. B. Du Bois, *The Souls of Black Folk* (New York: Barnes and Noble Classics, 2004), 5.

BIBLIOGRAPHY

Ammerman, Nancy. "Lived Religion." In *Emerging Trends in the Social and Behavioral Sciences: An Interdisciplinary, Searchable, and Linkable Resource*, 1–8. Hoboken, NJ: Wiley Online Library, 2015.

Anderson, Elijah. *Code of the Street: Decency, Violence, and the Moral Life of the Inner City*. New York: Norton, 2000.

——. *Streetwise: Race, Class, and Change in an Urban Community*. Chicago: University of Chicago Press, 1992.

Baker, William J. Introduction to *Basketball: Its Origin and Development*, by James Naismith. Lincoln: University of Nebraska Press, 1996.

Beck, Ulrich. "Laudatio." Speech at presentation of Ernst Bloch prize to Pierre Bourdieu. Ludwigshafen, November 1997.

Bidgood, Jess. "Violence Rises in Boston off the National Stage." *New York Times*, September 6, 2013.

Birth of a Nation. Directed by D. W. Griffith. 1915. New York: Kino on Video, 2002, DVD.

Bouissac, Paul. *Saussure: A Guide for the Perplexed*. New York: Continuum Books, 2010.

Bourdieu, Pierre. *Distinction*. Trans. Richard Nice. Cambridge, Mass.: Harvard University Press, 1984.

——. "The Forms of Capital." In *Handbook of Theory and Research for the Sociology of Education*, ed. John Richardson, 241–258. New York: Greenwood Press, 1986.

——. "Genesis and Structure of the Religious Field." *Comparative Social Research* 13 (1991): 1–44.

——. *The Logic of Practice*. Stanford, Calif.: Stanford University Press, 1990.

——. *Outline of a Theory of Practice*. Trans. Richard Nice. Cambridge: Cambridge University Press, 1977.

——. *Pascalian Meditations*. Trans. Richard Nice. Stanford, Calif.: Stanford University Press, 1997.

——. *The Weight of the World: Social Suffering in Contemporary Society*. Stanford, Calif.: Stanford University Press, 2000.

Bourdieu, Pierre, and Jean-Claude Passeron. *Reproduction in Education, Society, and Culture*. Trans. Richard Nice. London: Sage, 1990.

Bourdieu, Pierre, and Loïc J. D. Wacquant. *An Invitation to Reflexive Sociology*. Chicago: University of Chicago Press, 1992.

Braga, Anthony A., David Hureau, and Christopher Winship, "Losing Faith? Police, Black Churches, and the Resurgence of Youth Violence in Boston." *Ohio State Journal of Criminal Law* 6 (2008), http://moritzlaw.osu.edu/osjcl /Articles/Volume6_1/Braga-PDF.pdf.

Brooks, Scott N. *Black Men Can't Shoot*. Chicago: University of Chicago Press, 2009.

——. "City of Basketball Love: Philadelphia and the Nurturing of Black Male Hoop Dreams." *Journal of African American History* 96 (Fall 2011): 522–536.

——. "Fighting Like a Basketball Player: Basketball as a Strategy Against Social Disorganization." In *Against the Wall: Poor, Black, and Male*, ed. Elijah Anderson, 147–164. Philadelphia: University of Pennsylvania Press, 2008.

——. "Just a Dream? Structure, Power, and Agency in Basketball." In *Sport and Challenges to Racism*, ed. Jonathan Long and Karl Spracklen, 135–149. London: Palgrave Macmillan, 2011.

Brooks, Scott N., and Michael A. McKail, "A Theory of the Preferred Worker: A Structural Explanation for Black Male Dominance in Basketball," *Critical Sociology* 34 (2008): 369–387.

Buford May, Reuben A. *Living Through the Hoop: High School Basketball, Race, and the American Dream*. New York: New York University Press, 2007.

Bulhan, Hussein. *Frantz Fanon and the Psychology of Oppression*. New York: Plenum Press, 1985.

Caponi-Tabery, Gena. "Jump for Joy: Jump Blues, Dance, and Basketball in 1930s African America." In *Sports Matters: Race, Recreation, and Culture*, ed. John Bloom and Michael Nevin Willard, 39–74. New York: New York University Press, 2002.

"Chris Paul Pays Tribute to His Grandfather in 2002." *ESPN Sports Center Flashback*, May 8, 2008, https://www.youtube.com/watch?v=fxwyE5m44x4.

Cooke, Sam. "A Change Is Gonna Come." *Ain't That Good News*. RCA Victor LSP-2899, 1964, LP.

Cramer, Maria, and Brian R. Ballou, "Playing Scared: A Neighborhood Reflects as Teen Killed on Court Is Mourned," *Boston Globe*, May 12, 2010.

Daniel, Yvonne. *Dancing Wisdom: Embodied Knowledge in Haitian Vodou, Cuban Yoruba, and Bahian Candomble*. Urbana: University of Illinois Press, 2005.

Denzin, Norman. *Performance Ethnography: Critical Pedagogy and the Politics of Culture*. London: Sage, 2003.

Derrida, Jacques. *Specters of Marx: The State of the Debt, the Work of Mourning, and the New International*. Trans. Peggy Kamuf. New York: Routledge, 1994.

Devine-Eller, Audrey. "Rethinking Bourdieu on Race: A Critical Review of Cultural Capital and Habitus in the Sociology of Education Qualitative Literature." Presented at Rutgers University, New Brunswick, N.J., May 2, 2005.

Doin' It in the Park: Pick-Up Basketball, NYC. Directed by Bobbito Garcia and Kevin Couliau. New York: Goldcrest Films, 2012, DVD.

Du Bois, W. E. B. *The Souls of Black Folk*. New York: Barnes and Noble Classics, 2004.

Duneier, Mitchell. *Slim's Table: Race, Respectability, and Masculinity*. Chicago: University of Chicago Press, 1994.

Durkheim, Emile. *The Elementary Forms of Religious Life*. New York: Free Press, 1965.

Durkheim, Emile, and Marcel Mauss. *Primitive Classification*. Trans. Rodney Needham. Chicago: University of Chicago Press, 1967.

Dyson, Michael Eric. "Be Like Mike? Michael Jordan and the Pedagogy of Desire." In *Between Borders: Pedagogy and the Politics of Cultural Studies*, ed. Henry A. Giroux and Peter McLaren, 119–126. New York: Routledge, 1994.

Edwards, Harry. "The Black 'Dumb Jock': An American Sports Tragedy." *College Board Review* 131 (Spring 1984): 8–13.

——. *Revolt of the Black Athlete*. New York: Free Press: 1969.

——. "Sport Within the Veil: The Triumphs, Tragedies and Challenges of Afro-American Involvement." *Annals of the American Academy of Political and Social Science* 445 (September 1979): 116–127.

Eitle, T. M., and D. J. Eitle. "Race, Cultural Capital, and the Educational Effects of Participation in Sports." *Sociology of Education* 75 (2002): 123–146.

Ellison, Gregory C., II. "Late Stylin' in an Ill-Fitting Suit: Donald Capps' Artistic Approach to the Hopeful Self and Its Implications for Unacknowledged African American Young Men." *Pastoral Psychology* 58 (2009): 477–489.

——. *Cut Dead But Still Alive: Caring for African American Young Men* (Nashville, Tenn.: Abingdon Press, 2013).

Fathers of the Sport. Directed by Xavier Mitchell. Fayetteville, Ark.: Trace Entertainment LLC, 2008, DVD.

Finucane, Martin. "City Residents Reeling after Mattapan Slayings." *Boston Globe*, September 28, 2010.

Fluker, Clinton R. "Meet King Kong." Mellon Fellowship Paper. Morehouse and Spelman Colleges, Atlanta, Ga., May 2008.

Fluker, Walter E. "Cultural Asylums and the Jungles Planted in Them: The Exilic Condition of African American Males and the Black Church." Presented at Religious Practices in Global Contexts: "Religion, Conflict, and Peacemaking," at Boston University School of Theology, Spring 2011. Available at http://www.bu.edu/sth/files/2013/06/Fluker-Cultural-Asylums.pdf.

——. "Dangerous Memories and Redemptive Possibilities: Reflections on the Life and Work of Howard Thurman." *Critical Review of International Social and Political Philosophy* 7 (Winter 2004): 147–176.

Freud, Sigmund. *Mourning and Melancholia*. In *The Standard Edition of the Complete Psychological Works of Sigmund Freud, Volume XIV (1914–1916): On the History of the Psycho-Analytic Movement, Papers on Metapsychology, and Other Works*, 237–258. New York: Norton, 1976.

Gates, Henry Louis, Jr. "'The Blackness of Blackness': A Critique of the Sign and the Signifying Monkey." *Critical Inquiry* 9, no. 4 (1983): 686–723.

Geertz, Clifford. "'Deep Play: Notes on the Balinese Cockfight." *Daedalus* 134 (Winter 1972): 56–86.

Green, Ben. *Spinning the Globe: The Rise, Fall, and Return to Greatness of the Harlem Globetrotters*. New York: Amistad, 2006.

Griffin, Rachel Alicia. "The Disgrace of Commodification and the Shameful Convenience: A Critical Race Critique of the NBA." *Journal of Black Studies* 43, no. 2 (2012): 161–185.

Haiken, Melanie. "Racism May Speed Aging in African American Men." *Forbes*, January 7, 2014.

Hancock, Black. "Steppin' Out of Whiteness." *Ethnography* 6, no. 4 (2005): 427–461.

Harker, Richard, Cheleen Mahar, and Chris Wilkes, eds. *Introduction to the Work of Pierre Bourdieu: The Practice of Theory*. New York: St. Martin's Press, 1990.

Hawkins, Billy. "The Black Student Athlete: The Colonized Black Body." *Journal of African American Men* 1, no. 3 (1995/96): 23–35.

——. *The New Plantation: Black Athletes, College Sports, and Predominantly White NCAA Institutions*. New York: Palgrave Macmillan, 2013.

He Got Game. Directed by Spike Lee. Burbank, Calif.: Touchstone Pictures and Forty Acres & a Mule Filmworks, 1998, DVD.

Headley, Clevis. "Egological Investigations: A Comparative Study of African Existentialism and Western Existentialism." *C. L. R. James Journal* 10, no. 1 (2004): 73–105.

Heidegger, Martin. *Being and Time*. Trans. John Macquarrie and Edward Robinson. New York: Harper Perennial Modern Classics, 2008.

Henry, Paget. *Caliban's Reason: Introducing Afro-Caribbean Philosophy*. New York: Routledge, 2000.

Hoberman, John. *Darwin's Athletes: How Sport as Damaged Black America and Preserved the Myth of Race*. Boston: Houghton Mifflin, 1997.

Hopkins, Gerard Manley. "The Windhover: To Christ Our Lord." In *The Poems of Gerard Manley Hopkins*, ed. W. H. Gardner and N. H. Mackenzie. Oxford: Oxford University Press, 1967.

Horvat, Erin McNamara. "The Interactive Effects of Race and Class in Educational Research: Theoretical Insights from the Work of Pierre Bourdieu." *Penn GSE Perspectives on Urban Education* 2, no. 1 (2003): 1–25.

Husserl, Edmund. *Cartesian Meditations: An Introduction to Phenomenology.* Trans. Dorion Cairns. The Hague: Martinus Nijhoff Publishers, 1977.

James, William. *The Variety of Religious Experience: A Study in Human Nature.* 1902. New York: Random House, 1999.

Jealous, Benjamin. "Zimmerman Verdict: Keep Fighting," *Skanner,* July 16, 2013, http://www.theskanner.com/article/Zimmerman-Verdict-Keep-Fighting -2013-07-16.

Johnson, Claude. *Black Fives: The Alpha Physical Culture Club's Pioneering African American Basketball Team, 1904–1923.* Greenwich, Conn.: Black Fives Publishing, 2012.

Jones, Jim. "Rain." *Pray IV Reign.* Columbia / Ether Boy 88697 19376, 2009, CD.

Jones, Richard A. "Race and Revisability." *Journal of Black Studies* 35, no. 5 (2005): 612–632.

King Kong. Directed by Peter Jackson. Universal City, Calif.: Universal Pictures, 2005, DVD.

Labov, William. *Language in the Inner City: Studies in the Black English Vernacular.* Philadelphia: University of Pennsylvania Press, 1973.

Lamont, Michele, and Annette Lareau. "Cultural Capital, Allusions, Gaps, and Glissandos in Recent Theoretical Developments." *Sociological Theory* 6 (1998): 152–168.

Lareau, Annette, and Erin McNamara Horvat. "Moments of Social Inclusion and Exclusion: Race, Class, and Cultural Capital in Family-School Relationships." *Sociology of Education* 72 (1999): 37–53.

Leary, Joy DeGruy. *Post Traumatic Slave Syndrome: America's Legacy of Enduring Injury and Healing.* Milwaukie, Ore.: Uptone Press, 2005.

Leeuw, Gerardus van der. *Religion in Essence and Manifestation.* Trans. J. E. Turner. London: George Allen and Unwin, 1938.

Leonard, David. "The Decline of the Black Athlete: An Online Exclusive: Extended Interview with Harry Edwards." *Colorlines,* April 20, 2000, http://colorlines.com /archives/2000/04/the_decline_of_the_black_athletean_online_exclusive _extended_interview_with_harry_edwards.html.

——. "The Real Color of Money: Controlling Black Bodies in the NBA." *Journal of Sport and Social Issues* 30, no. 2 (May 2006): 158–179.

Long, Charles H. "African American Religion in the United States of America: An Interpretive Essay." *Nova Religio: The Journal of Alternative and Emergent Religions* 7, no. 1 (2003): 11–27.

——. *Significations: Signs, Symbols, and Images in the Interpretations of Religion.* Philadelphia: Fortress Press, 1986.

Mallozzi, Vincent. *Asphalt Gods: An Oral History of Rucker Park*. New York: Doubleday, 2003.

Marshall, Tulaine S., and Jacqui Conrad, eds. "State of Black Boston 2011: Good News and Good Work to Be Done." Urban League of Eastern Massachusetts, 2011, https://docs.google.com/file/d/oBx93m3UUyugcbHV5VkN2YkdwLUE /edit?pli=1.

Maykut, Pamela, and Richard Morehouse. *Beginning Qualitative Research: A Philosophic and Practical Guide*. Washington, D.C.: Falmer Press, 1994.

McFadden, James P. "PBHA Students Grieve Killing of Local Teen." *Harvard Crimson*, December, 15, 1997.

Meissner, W. W. *Freud and Psychoanalysis*. Notre Dame, Ind.: University of Notre Dame Press, 2000.

Merleau-Ponty, Maurice. *Phenomenology of Perception*. Trans. Donald A. Landes. New York: Routledge, 2012.

Miller, Chuck. "The 2011 Louis Saunders Memorial Basketball Tournament." Timesunion.com, August 3, 2011, http://blog.timesunion.com/chuckmiller /the-2011-louis-saunders-memorial-basketball-tournament/9656/.

Mitchell, Mozella G. *Spiritual Dynamics of Howard Thurman's Theology*. Bristol, Ind.: Wyndham Hall Press, 1985.

Mitchell-Kernan, Claudia. "Signifying, Loud-Talking, and Marking." In *Signifyin(g), Sanctifyin', and Slam Dunking*, ed. Gena Dagel Caponi, 309–330. Amherst: University of Massachusetts Press, 1999.

Mjagkij, Nina. *Light in the Darkness: African Americans and the YMCA, 1852–1946*. Lexington: University Press of Kentucky, 2003.

Morris, Gay. "Bourdieu, the Body, and Graham's Post-War Dance." *Dance Research* 19 (October 2001): 52–82.

Morrison, Toni. *Beloved*. New York: Vintage, 2004.

Mudimbe, V. Y. "Reading and Teaching Pierre Bourdieu." *Transition* 61 (1993): 144–160.

Murphy, Joseph. *Working the Spirit: Ceremonies of the African Diaspora*. Boston: Beacon Press, 1994.

Naismith, James. *Basketball: Its Origin and Development*. Lincoln: University of Nebraska Press, 1996.

Noel, James. *Black Religion and the Imagination of Matter in the Atlantic World*. New York: Palgrave Macmillan, 2009.

Obama, Barack. *Dreams from My Father: A Story of Race and Inheritance*. New York: Broadway Books, 2004.

Oliver, William. "'The Streets': An Alternative Black Male Socialization Institution." *Journal of Black Studies* 36, no. 6 (2006): 918–937.

On the Shoulders of Giants. Directed by Deborah Morales. S.I.: Union Productions, 2011, DVD.

Otto, Rudolf. *The Idea of the Holy.* Trans. John Harvey. New York: Oxford University Press, 1958.

"Perceived Racism May Impact Black Americans' Mental Health." Press release. American Psychological Association, November 16, 2011, http://www.apa.org/news/press/releases/2011/11/racism.aspx.

Pinn, Anthony. "Black Bodies in Pain and Ecstasy: Terror, Subjectivity, and the Nature of Black Religion." *Nova Religio-Journal of Alternative and Emergent Religions* 7, no. 1 (2003): 76–89.

——. *Terror and Triumph: The Nature of Black Religion.* Minneapolis, Minn.: Fortress Press, 2003.

Prothero, Stephen. *God Is Not One.* New York: HarperOne, 2010.

Putney, Clifford. *Muscular Christianity: Manhood and Sports in Protestant America, 1880–1920.* Cambridge, Mass.: Harvard University Press, 2001.

Raboteau, Albert J. *Slave Religion: The 'Invisible Institution' in the Antebellum South.* New York: Oxford University Press, 2004.

Reed-Danahay, Deborah. *Locating Bourdieu.* Bloomington: Indiana University Press, 2005.

Rhoden, William C. *Forty Million Dollar Slaves: The Rise, Fall, and Redemption of the Black Athlete.* New York: Three Rivers Press, 2006.

Richardson, Joseph B., Jr. "Beyond the Playing Field: Coaches as Social Capital for Inner-City Adolescent African American Males." *Journal of African American Studies* 16 (2012): 171–194.

Robbins, Derek. *The Work of Pierre Bourdieu: Recognizing Society.* Boulder, Colo.: Westview, 1991.

Sartre, Jean-Paul. *Being and Nothingness.* Trans. Hazel E. Barnes. New York: Pocket Books, 1966.

Saussure, Ferdinand de. *Course in General Linguistics.* Trans. Roy Harris. Chicago: Open Court, 1998.

Scott, James C. *Domination and the Arts of Resistance: Hidden Transcripts.* New Haven, Conn.: Yale University Press, 1990.

Scriven, Joseph C. "What a Friend We Have in Jesus." In *Pilgrim Hymnal*, 335. Boston: Pilgrim Press, 1968.

Shakib, Sohalia, and Philip Veliz. "Race, Sport and Social Support: A Comparison Between African American and White Youth's Perceptions of Social Support for Sport Participation." *International Review of the Sociology of Sport* 48, no. 3 (2012): 295–317.

Sharlet, Jeff. *Sweet Heaven When I Die: Faith, Faithlessness, and the Country in Between.* New York: Norton, 2011.

Simons, Herbert D. "Race and Penalized Sports Behavior." *International Review for the Sociology of Sport* 38, no. 1 (2003): 5–22.

Smalls, Biggie. "Things Done Changed." The Notorious B.I.G. *Ready to Die.* Bad Boy Entertainment, SXBS-7006, 1994, CD.

Some, Malidoma Patrice. *Ritual: Power, Healing, and Community*. New York: Penguin Books, 1997.

Stepto, Robert B. *From Behind the Veil: A Study of Afro-American Narrative*. Urbana: University of Illinois Press, 1991.

Sullivan, Robert. "Lebron James and Gisele Bundchen: Dream Team." *Vogue*, April 2008.

Tettenborn, Éva. "Melancholia as Resistance in Contemporary African American Literature." *MELUS* 31, no. 3 (Fall 2006): 101–121.

Thurman, Howard. Howard Thurman Collection. Howard Gotlieb Archival Research Center. Boston University.

——. *The Inward Journey*. Richmond, Ind.: Friends United Press, 1971.

——. *A Strange Freedom: The Best of Howard Thurman on Religious Experience and Public Life*. Ed. Walter E. Fluker and Catherine Tumber. Boston: Beacon Press, 1999.

Training Day. Directed by Antoine Fuqua. Burbank Calif.: Warner Brothers, 2001, DVD.

Tunstall, Dwayne A. "Taking Africana Existential Philosophy of Education Seriously." *Philosophical Studies in Education* 39 (2008): 46–55.

van Gennep, Arnold. *The Rites of Passage*. Chicago: University of Chicago Press, 1961.

Wacquant, Loïc. *Body and Soul: Notebooks of an Apprentice Boxer*. New York: Oxford University Press, 2004.

White Men Can't Jump. Directed by Ron Shelton. Beverly Hills, Calif.: Twentieth-Century Fox Film Corporation, 1992, DVD.

Wideman, John Edgar. *Hoop Roots*. Boston: Houghton Mifflin, 2003.

Wilkerson, Isabel. *The Warmth of Other Suns: The Epic Story of America's Great Migration*. New York: Random House, 2010.

Wilson, William Julius. *The Truly Disadvantaged: The Inner City, the Underclass, and Public Policy*. Chicago: University of Chicago Press, 1987.

Winnicott, Donald W. *Playing and Reality*. New York: Basic Books, 2005.

Withers, Bill. "Grandma's Hands." *Just as I Am*. Sussex SXBS-7006, 1971, LP.

Wittgenstein, Ludwig. *Tractatus Logico-Philosophicus*. Trans. D. F. Pears and B. F. McGuiness. London: Routledge and Kegan Paul, 1963.

Woodbine, Onaje. "An Invisible Institution: A Functional Approach to Religion in Sports in Wounded African American Communities." In *The Black Church and Hip Hop Culture: Toward Bridging the Generational Divide*, ed. Emmett G. Price III, 173–184. Lanham, Md.: Scarecrow Press, 2011.

——. "Why I'm Quitting Basketball." *Yale Alumni Magazine*, November 2000.

Young, Hershini. *Haunting Capital: Memory, Text, and the Black Diasporic Body*. Hanover, N.H.: Dartmouth University Press, 2005.

INDEX

CPSIA information can be obtained
at www.ICGtesting.com
Printed in the USA
LVHW092021050821
694635LV00001B/121